TAMING CHAOS

"*Taming CHAOS* is an excellent and appealing way for students and families to learn about risk and making good decisions."

—**Sonia Levitin**, *Award Winning*, German American Novelist, Young Adult Author and Holocaust Survivor

"Gary Miller's analysis of risk management is spot on. The book was written for teens, but it may interest college students too!"

—**M. Moshe Porat**, Ph.D., CPCU, Dean, Fox School of Business, Temple University

"Adolescence is the frontier during which children transition from dreamers to doers. Unlike adults; however, teens do not have the brain development necessary to create and stick to concrete decisions in their best interest. *Taming CHAOS* provides young adult readers with a prescriptive decision-making tool that is woven into the fabric of this delightful novel about decision-making and managing risk to adopt a rescued dog. *Taming CHAOS*: charming, age-appropriate, relevant for young teens who struggle with decision-making at the onset of carving out their unique path in life."

—**Jeannie Hofmann**, English Teacher, *Teacher of the Year*, Upper Moreland High School, Montgomery County, PA

"As a current Middle School Principal and former High School Math Teacher, *Taming CHAOS* embraces all aspects of adolescent social, emotional, quantitative & analytical development throughout its highly enjoyable story. All School Districts should adopt this excellent thought provoking book into their Character Education & Math Curriculums!"

—**Adam Slavin**, Middle School Principal, Upper Merion Area School District, Montgomery County, PA

TAMING
CHAOS

A PARABLE ON DECISION MAKING

GARY R. MILLER

New York

TAMING CHAOS
A PARABLE ON DECISION MAKING

Published in New York, New York, by Morgan James Publishing. Morgan James and The Entrepreneurial Publisher are trademarks of Morgan James, LLC.
www.MorganJamesPublishing.com

The Morgan James Speakers Group can bring authors to your live event. For more information or to book an event visit The Morgan James Speakers Group at www.TheMorganJamesSpeakersGroup.com.

Shelfie

A **free** eBook edition is available
with the purchase of this print book.

CLEARLY PRINT YOUR NAME ABOVE IN UPPER CASE

Instructions to claim your free eBook edition:
1. Download the Shelfie app for Android or iOS
2. Write your name in **UPPER CASE** above
3. Use the Shelfie app to submit a photo
4. Download your eBook to any device

ISBN 978-1-68350-060-5 paperback
ISBN 978-1-68350-061-2 eBook
ISBN 978-1-68350-062-9 hardcover
Library of Congress Control Number:
2016906955

Cover Design by:
Rachel Lopez
www.r2cdesign.com

Interior Design by:
Bonnie Bushman
The Whole Caboodle Graphic Design

In an effort to support local communities, raise awareness and funds, Morgan James Publishing donates a percentage of all book sales for the life of each book to Habitat for Humanity Peninsula and Greater Williamsburg.

Get involved today! Visit
www.MorganJamesBuilds.com

I would like to thank those that supported and encouraged me. You all have been such a great team to work with and without your support this book would not have been possible. With gratitude and love. God bless each one of you!

To my wife Carol

To my children Matthew, Jody, Nicholas, Grace, Anne and Adam

To my grandchildren Westin, Hudson, Graceyn, Jordan, Luke, Mackenna and Drew

To my mother Mary Lou and my father and business partner Raymond Miller, Jr.

To my friend Jeanne Hofmann

To my nephew Danny Ciurczak

To my business associate Paul Prizer

CHAPTER 1

Hurry up, we're going to be late!"

"We are not!"

Jimmy stood up on his pedals to get more speed, swerving around his sister Carly and pulling ahead of her on the sidewalk. It was 8:17 a.m. on a Monday morning, and the two of them had exactly thirteen minutes left to get to school, lock up their bikes, and be in their seats before the bell rang.

"We should have left earlier!" Carly called.

Jimmy pedaled furiously, trying to put some distance between himself and his sister. She was *always* bossing him around. And half the time she wasn't even right about it!

They didn't need any extra time. After all, they'd been biking to the same K-through-eight school for years now; Jimmy had boiled the trip down to a science. Once they had

1

their backpacks and shoes on, it was two minutes to get their bikes out of the garage and say goodbye to Mom and Dad, eight minutes to ride to school, and three minutes to lock their bikes on the rack outside school.

So today, that left them *two whole minutes* to get to their classrooms. Carly was being so annoying. They had more than enough time.

Jimmy thought he'd gotten far ahead of Carly—but no such luck. He was in seventh grade and she was in eighth, and they were just about the same size, but Carly could put some power behind her pedals when she wanted to. She pulled up alongside Jimmy.

"Jimmy. It's the *first day of school*. I wanted to say hi to my friends and set up my new locker. Now I'll be lucky to make the bell. If you hadn't spent all morning on your phone playing that stupid Grumpy Crows game—"

"Ugh!" Jimmy exclaimed. "You didn't *have* to wait for me. Nobody *made* you. You could've left when you were ready."

For a moment, Carly was stunned into silence. It hadn't even occurred to her to leave for school without her brother. Ever since their parents had given them permission to ride to school alone when she started fifth grade and he started fourth, the two of them had always gone together. The only time she'd ever biked to school without Jimmy was when he had the chickenpox—and that had been *the worst*. What was the point of riding to school alone?

"I wasn't going to just leave you!" Carly started, but something on Jimmy's face made her stop. His head was cocked to the side, and he was listening—listening to something or someone other than Carly.

This was unusual. Jimmy and Carly spent most of their time bickering—bickering in a loving, sibling kind of way—and both of them cared more than they'd ever admit about being right. If Jimmy stopped paying attention in the middle of a spat with Carly, there was something seriously wrong.

All of a sudden, Jimmy squeezed the brakes on his six-speed bike. He squeezed hard. Carly didn't have a second to react. All she saw was a flash of lime green metal and spokes beside her as Jimmy stopped short, and then her momentum carried her way ahead of him. She screeched her teal six-speed to a halt, her helmet rattling around her ears.

"Did you hear that?" Jimmy shouted to his sister. In an instant, their fight had disappeared from his mind. Jimmy was standing astride his bike, peering off into the bushes that lined the sidewalk. Behind the bushes, a slope led to a dense little forest that bordered the northern side of Carly and Jimmy's neighborhood.

Carly felt her heart thrum inside her ribcage. She jumped off her bike and dropped it in the grass, running back to where Jimmy was standing stock-still.

"What's wrong? Jimmy! What's going on?"

"Shhh!" Jimmy hissed. "I'm *listening*. Don't you hear that?"

The two of them stood very quietly for a moment, their chins tilted toward the forest. And then, Carly heard it—the sound that had made Jimmy stop. A rustling of leaves, a crackling of twigs, and then a low, long, mournful groan.

Jimmy and Carly looked at each other wide-eyed. Very slowly, very quietly, Carly took a step toward the sound.

"Carly?" Jimmy whispered, alarmed. "What are you doing?"

Carly gave Jimmy a warning look. They knew each other well enough that all she had to do was raise her eyebrows and catch his eye to communicate: "Keep it down."

But Jimmy was too worried to obey.

"Carly," he whispered again. "You can't go in there; we don't know what that is."

Carly, who was already making her way through the low bushes toward the tree line, turned and looked back at Jimmy.

"It sounds like someone's hurt. We have to go see. They might need help."

Jimmy hesitated. Carly was right—it *did* sound like someone was hurt. Or *something*? The foliage was so dense that neither of them could make anything out.

Just then, in the brief moment that Jimmy and Carly paused, the leaves rustled again and, again, they heard that plaintive moan.

Jimmy threw down the kickstand of his bike and reached out to catch Carly's arm and hold her back, but she was too quick. In three short strides, she had made her way to the tree line and was squatting down to part the branches and leaves of the underbrush and peer inside. Jimmy didn't have time to think. Carly might be crazy, but he wasn't going to let her get into any scrapes alone. He caught up with her quickly and knelt down.

At first, the underbrush was too shadowy to see anything. And then, both Jimmy and Carly caught sight of them at the same time—two black eyes gleaming in the darkness. Suddenly, a flash of white teeth and a snarl. They saw jaws open wide and snap shut with a harsh, grating sound.

Jimmy and Carly jerked backwards. And then, to Carly's utter consternation, Jimmy leaned forward and parted the branches with his hands. He was full of contradictions, that brother of hers. Just when she thought she had him pegged as an over-cautious over-thinker, he went and did something braver and bolder than she could have imagined.

They held their breath as they peered silently at the animal in the shadows, waiting for their eyes to adjust.

Was it some kind of wild beast? Was it even an animal they could identify? At first it actually seemed like something out of the fantasy novels they liked to trade back and forth, reading again and again until the spines were cracked and the pages hopelessly dog-eared.

Unbidden, the word "werewolf" bubbled up in Carly's mind. She had to suck in a huge breath and hold it to keep her imagination from running wild. She knew full well there was no such thing as werewolves in real life. But then . . . what *was* this creature she was looking at?

It was massive. It was lying on its belly, enormous head and long, pointed snout resting on its forepaws. But even with its belly to the ground, it was huge, a great black mound of fur and stench.

Silently, Jimmy calculated to himself that if the creature were standing up, its head would reach well above his chest— and Jimmy was tall for his age.

Its coloring seemed to be a sort of charcoal gray, but it was hard to tell because its long, straggly fur was so matted and clumped. Long strands of fur were stuck together in thick snarls. As her eyes adjusted to the dim light, Carly realized with a sinking feeling that the fur was clinging together because of some kind of dark, congealed wetness. The animal was streaked with dried blood.

"It's hurt," Jimmy whispered.

Carly nodded. For a moment, the two of them were very silent and still, watching the creature. It shifted uneasily in its hideout, and then again, pulled back its upper lip to show its sharp front teeth and let out a rumbling growl.

The animal lifted its head off its paws, snarling, and pushed its snout forward toward Jimmy and Carly. They drew back quickly, and Jimmy gave a little gasp. But they weren't in any danger. No sooner had the creature lunged forward than it sank again onto its belly, exhausted. It was in too much pain and too weak to attack.

Carly and Jimmy exchanged a glance. In the brief instant that the creature had risen to try to lunge forward, it had become clear to both of them that this was no mystical beast. This was no werewolf. It was just a dog. A *huge* dog, sure—but just a dog.

The dog wriggled and moaned again, and as it did, Carly and Jimmy heard the clanking of metal. There was a rusted, broken chain hanging loosely from its neck.

"What do you think happened to it?" Carly breathed.

"Look at that chain," Jimmy said. "It must have run away from someplace."

"Yeah. I wonder if it broke the chain itself. It must be really strong."

Jimmy nodded wordlessly. He was looking at one of the dog's forelegs, which was bent at a strange angle underneath it. The leg looked broken. Had the dog been abused and beaten? Had it been hit by a car? Or maybe both?

In any case, it was clear to both Jimmy and Carly that the dog had been badly mistreated—and that it was in terrible trouble.

After a long silence, Jimmy asked, his voice breaking slightly with emotion, "Do you think it's going to be okay?"

Carly shook her head. "I don't know," she said honestly. "Maybe it's dying."

"What do we do?" Jimmy said, more to himself than to his sister. It wasn't so much a question as a sigh of despair. As aggressive and dangerous as this dog seemed, it was hurt and obviously scared. Jimmy felt his heart go out to the creature.

Carly stood up and brushed the grass off her jeans. She was back to business, ready to take charge as usual.

"We have to do *something*," she said. "We're already late for school—on the *first day*. So . . . either we leave right now and hope we don't get into too much trouble. Or, we stay here and help—and definitely get in trouble."

For a moment, Carly held Jimmy's gaze. And then, in the same instant, they nodded. They couldn't just leave the dog here to die. They had to try to help.

"Let's call the police," Jimmy said. "They'll know what to do."

"Good idea," Carly said, already pulling her cell phone out of her pocket. In a crisp, older-than-her-age tone, Carly explained to the dispatcher where they were and what shape the dog was in, and within minutes, she had been transferred to animal control.

Jimmy watched anxiously as she talked the animal control operator through the dog's condition. A shadow passed across Carly's face as she paused and listened.

"Okay . . ." she said slowly. Then she cupped a hand over her phone and murmured to Jimmy, "She says it'll take them at least an hour to get here."

Jimmy felt his heart drop into his shoes. It was clear that Carly was thinking the same thing he was. Being an hour or more late to school on the very first day? It was unheard of.

Just at that moment, the dog let out another moan. It was suffering.

Carly and Jimmy locked eyes. Without speaking, they agreed.

Carly brought the phone back up to her ear. "Okay. We'll stay here with the dog to make sure nothing happens. I'll call you back if there's any change," she said matter-of-factly. Sometimes Jimmy could hardly believe Carly was his sister—she sounded so much like their mom that he almost wondered if Carly was actually a miniature replica of her.

Carly and Jimmy sat down in the grass together a safe distance from the dog.

"Well," Carly said. "We've made our bed. Now we have to lie in it."

Jimmy couldn't help smiling. There was Mom's voice coming out of Carly's mouth again.

"We're definitely going to be in trouble," Jimmy said. "So . . . I guess we better make it worth it. Do you think we should do something to make the dog more comfortable?"

Carly nodded. "Of course. But what? I don't think we should try to touch it. It's weak, but if we get too close, I'm sure it would bite us."

Jimmy's eyes lit up. "It's probably hungry!" He exclaimed. He unslung his backpack from his shoulders, unzipped it, and pulled his lunchbox out.

"What do you think it would eat?" He asked, rustling through the lunch his mother had lovingly packed that morning. "Not a yogurt cup. Probably not an apple . . . bologna sandwich?"

"Give it a shot," Carly agreed.

Jimmy pulled a triangle of bologna sandwich out of its Ziploc baggie. Gently, he tossed the sandwich to the dog.

It was as if he'd thrown gold to a miser. The dog fell on the sandwich and devoured it in two gulps.

Carly and Jimmy looked at each other, eyebrows raised.

"Poor thing probably hasn't eaten in days," Carly murmured.

"Do you think it had an owner?" Jimmy said. "Maybe they didn't even feed it."

The two of them sat in silence for a moment. They didn't want to admit it, but they both were afraid of the beast. It was obviously on edge—and willing to defend itself. And it had clearly been so mistreated that it saw everything as a threat. This was not a sweet, fluffy puppy.

But this was also an innocent animal that had been treated badly. It wasn't its fault if it was on the defensive. It was hurt and terrified. And it might even be dying.

Just then, there was a screech of tires on the sidewalk behind Carly and Jimmy. They turned to see who had arrived, just as a voice called out to them.

"What're you doing?"

A tall, stocky boy had ridden up on a shiny, midnight blue ten-speed bike. He was leaning with one foot on the sidewalk, watching them. Neither Carly nor Jimmy recognized him. He had close-cropped blond hair, a full, freckled face, and was squinting at them in the sunlight.

"Are you guys, like, cutting school?" The boy demanded. He sounded more accusative than inquisitive.

Carly and Jimmy looked at each other. They didn't quite know what to say. Technically, they *were* cutting school. But not on purpose. Well . . . not really.

The boy dropped his bike in the grass and strode over. As he approached, the dog lifted its head. The thick, frizzy hair stood up on the back of its neck. It snapped and gave a throaty bark.

The boy peered for a moment into the thick brush at the dog, then sprang back warily.

"What the heck?" The boy exclaimed. Then he whirled on Jimmy and Carly, his eyes narrowing. "What are you guys *doing* with that thing?"

"It's hurt," Carly said frankly. "We called animal control so we can try to help it."

The boy threw back his head and let out a sharp laugh that sounded uncannily like the dog's growl.

"That's so stupid," he said. "That dog is messed up, man," he continued, turning dismissively from Carly to look at Jimmy. "If you want to help it, you should just find a way to put it out of its misery."

Jimmy felt his jaw drop unconsciously. All he could do was gape at the boy, open-mouthed. Carly was equally gobsmacked.

"*What?*" She said finally.

The boy snorted, turned his back on them, and walked back to his bike.

"I guess you're too scared," he called over his shoulder. He picked up his bike and swung his leg over it.

"Whatever," he said. "I thought you guys might actually be doing something fun. Good luck with your wittle puppy-wuppy."

He pushed his foot down on the pedal and began to coast away. As they watched him recede down the street, his voice echoed behind him.

"See you later, losers!"

CHAPTER 2

Carly was lying on her back in the grass, staring up at the passing clouds, when she heard the rumble of a vehicle pulling up alongside her and Jimmy. They both sat bolt upright.

They had been waiting for just over an hour, taking turns checking on the dog from time to time. It had been a pretty rough wait. The dog never got used to their presence, and every time they looked in to make sure it was still breathing, the hair on its neck stood on end and it bared its teeth. Finally, they had decided that they were making it too nervous by checking, so they'd decided to give it some space and wait for animal control further away from the trees, where their voices wouldn't carry and spook the dog.

Carly and Jimmy both stood, brushing loose leaves and blades of grass from their jeans. A large, white van had just pulled up. A black paw print was stamped on its windowless side, along with the words "County Animal Control" in dark red block letters. The van rumbled and sputtered for a moment before the engine choked to silence.

"Howdy!" A deep voice called, and a moment later, an animal control specialist came around the front of the van to greet Carly and Jimmy. "You kids call about a big stray dog in the bushes? Might be injured? Kinda mean?"

Carly and Jimmy both nodded wordlessly. They both shared the same characteristic of sometimes getting a little shy when they met a new adult. And this man wasn't exactly unintimidating. He was *very* tall—Jimmy figured he was at least three or four inches taller than their dad. He had a thick head of brown hair and an even thicker beard. His shoulders were broad and he had a slight paunch on his large frame.

He was dressed in an official-looking navy blue jumpsuit. The same paw print that was stamped on the side of his van was embroidered on the front chest pocket of his uniform. Jimmy was vaguely reminded of the folklore of Paul Bunyan the lumberjack he'd read in school.

The silence only lasted a split second before Carly remembered her manners and put out a friendly hand, just as their parents had taught them.

"My name is Carly, and this is my brother Jim," she said. "We did call. We think the dog is hurt."

"I'm Hank," said the lumberjack—or, the animal control specialist. He took Carly's hand in his powerful grip and gave it a hearty pump. Suddenly, both Carly and Jimmy felt at ease. They both appreciated when adults just acted naturally instead of talking down to them.

"Say," Hank said, "shouldn't you two be in school?"

Carly and Jimmy hesitated for a split second.

"We're going straight there after this," Carly said, deciding to tell the truth. "We found the dog and didn't want to leave it alone while you were on your way to help us."

Hank raised a thick, dark eyebrow and nodded slowly. "All right," he said. "Then we better wrap this up quick. You two need to be on your way."

Carly and Jimmy showed Hank the place in the trees where the dog was lying, and Hank crouched down.

As soon as he did, the dog barked and snapped, raising its head off its forepaws and struggling to come to standing. It tried weakly to wriggle backward into the underbrush away from Hank. Clearly, something about Hank scared it even more than Carly and Jimmy did.

Hank's brow creased with concern and he spoke in a soft voice.

"Oh boy," he said. "You two were right to call. It's definitely injured—and very scared."

"It's gotten worse!" Jimmy blurted. "It never tried to get away from us."

"Well," Hank said with a smile, "I'm bigger than you are, so it thinks it has more reason to be afraid of me. The sad thing is," he continued, watching the dog carefully, "we don't see an animal react like this unless it's got some reason to feel skittish. I'm sorry to tell you guys, but this dog has probably been mistreated."

Just then, the dog snapped again, and turned its head quickly as if it were searching for an escape. As it did, the broken chain that hung from its neck swung around and rattled.

"Aha," Hank said grimly. "Looks like this dog definitely didn't come from a good home."

Then he pointed to the dog's right foreleg, which Carly and Jimmy had already noticed was injured. "But I doubt a person did that. If I had to guess, I'd say it's been hit by a car. It's not going to run off anywhere with that injury, but I will still have to use a catch pole."

Jimmy bristled unconsciously. "You're not going to hurt it, are you?"

Hank gave both Jimmy and Carly a reassuring smile. "I won't hurt it a bit," he promised. "But the dog still won't like it. I'm gonna ask the two of you to stand back over there." Hank pointed toward the sidewalk a safe distance removed from the dog.

Then he got up, went back to the van, and threw open its backdoors. He rummaged around for a moment, gathering supplies, and then returned to the tree line with a large, wire cage and a long pole with a loop of cord at its end. Carly and Jimmy hung back where Hank had told them to wait, watching.

"See this?" Hank called to them, holding up the pole. "It's called a catch pole. I'll just loop the cord around the dog's neck, and then the pole helps me control it and keep it a safe distance away from my body in case it tries to bite."

Hank set the cage down in the grass not far from where the dog was cowering and opened its door so that it was ready and waiting.

Then, he moved swiftly and skillfully. Before Carly and Jimmy even knew what had happened, there was a rustling in the trees, a long, savage growl, and the dog was sliding on its belly out from the underbrush with the catch pole's cord around its neck. Hank murmured gently to the dog the whole time.

"Okay, come on buddy, that's it," he breathed.

Once the dog was clear of the trees, it staggered to its feet. It couldn't put weight on its injured forepaw, so it loped along on three paws, continuing to bare its teeth. Its ears were pressed flat against its head, and its eyes were wide and rolling with terror.

Very slowly, very gently, Hank drew the dog through the open door of the cage, careful not to pull it off-balance so that it wouldn't have to use its broken leg. Once the dog was inside, he gracefully released the catchpole from its neck and closed the cage door, latching it firmly.

"Any chance you two could give me a hand with this?" Hank asked. "Looks like we got a pretty hefty pup here."

Carly and Jimmy approached nervously. With impressive strength, Hank hoisted the cage—even though the dog inside probably weighed almost as much as Carly or Jimmy—and, with the two kids supporting the opposite end of the cage, they carried it to the van together. Inside the cage, the dog shifted and moaned anxiously, but it did not try to stand. An instant later, cage, dog, and all had disappeared into the back of the van and the doors were firmly closed.

"That's it, guys," Hank said. "I'll get this guy over to the shelter, but you can rest easy now. You did a really good thing for that animal."

"But—" Carly started, incredulous. "What happens now? I mean, how do we find out if the dog's going to be okay?"

"Oh," Hank said, surprised. "Well . . ." He looked from Carly to Jimmy and back again, clearly a little moved. "To be honest, people don't usually ask me that question. Usually they just want to make sure stray animals that might be dangerous are out of their neighborhoods."

Hank took a breath. "I'll be honest with you kids, because you've already proved that you're mature and thoughtful by looking out for this dog this morning. The dog has a chance, but it's only a chance. I'm going to take the dog to the county shelter. They get a lot of animals there—more than they can take care of, and so they do euthanize animals that they can't place in homes quickly."

Jimmy's heart lurched. He looked at his sister and knew instantly that she was feeling the same mixture of dread and sadness. He mustered his most adult voice and asked, "Is there anything we can do to help?"

Hank pursed his lips grimly. "The people who run the shelter would love to keep every animal, but they're just not able to. It's better for them to concentrate on finding homes for the animals they *can* save. So, hopefully there's a family that notices this dog at the shelter—and soon. That's the best chance the dog has."

Hank's words hung heavily in the air for a moment. Finally, he continued, "No matter what happens to this dog, you did a good thing today. It almost definitely would have died scared and in pain and alone if you hadn't called us."

He put out his hand and shook Carly's hand and then Jimmy's, once again giving them a steady, respectful gaze, like they were adults and not middle-schoolers with their hearts in their throats.

Carly put on her Mom-like voice again. "Thanks so much for helping us," she told Hank.

"Yeah," Jimmy agreed, nodding. "Thank you."

With that, Hank climbed back into the van, and Carly and Jimmy stood on the sidewalk watching with long faces as he pulled away.

As the van disappeared around the corner at the end of the lane, Jimmy walked slowly back to his bike, and Carly followed. She glanced at her watch as they went.

"Ugh," she murmured. "We missed first period completely. We are going to be in so much trouble."

Jimmy groaned. Neither one of them had ever even dreamed of cutting school. On the rare occasions that they were late, they usually had a *really* good excuse—and a note from their parents to back it up. Neither of them even knew *how* to be this late. Should they report to the front office before going to class? Should they call their parents before going on to school to explain what had happened?

And then suddenly it hit Jimmy: the awful feeling in his belly had much less to do with being late for the first day of school—as unpleasant as that was—and much more to do with what Hank had just told them about the dog.

"I don't even care about school right now!" He blurted. "I just can't believe the shelter might kill the dog. I thought we were helping it!"

As soon as Jimmy spoke, Carly realized that he'd voiced exactly her feelings. She took a deep breath, resisting the temptation to sink completely into sorrow.

"We *did* help it," she reminded Jimmy gently. "You heard what Hank said. Even if they euthanize the dog, it's better than it dying in pain all by itself out here. And it does have a chance at the shelter."

"A tiny chance," Jimmy muttered.

"Yeah," Carly nodded. She had to admit it—he was right. "But it's a chance." She paused for a moment. "Look, we made the choice to help it, and at least for now, there's nothing more we can do. We have to focus on the rest of the day now. And then—" an idea came to her in the middle of her sentence "—when we get home from school, let's ask Mom and Dad if we can go to the shelter and check on the dog."

Jimmy gasped. "Oh my gosh!" He exclaimed. "That's genius, Carly!"

She shrugged knowingly. "Of course it is."

Feeling heartened, they both swung back onto their bikes and started to pedal in the direction of the school.

"Do you think we should call Mom and Dad and tell them what happened?" Jimmy asked as they rode.

"I think we're really, really late already," Carly said. "We should just get to school, be honest with our teachers, and get back on track as fast as we can. And then we can explain to Mom and Dad when we get home."

"Won't they be mad?" Jimmy asked. "What if the school already called them?"

Carly swallowed. She hadn't thought of that.

"The school probably already *did* call them," she said.

Jimmy knew Carly was right.

"Well . . . in that case," he said slowly, "I guess we really should just get to school as fast as we can. Hopefully Mom and Dad will understand when we get home and tell them what happened."

"Right," said Carly.

With that, they pedaled in subdued silence the rest of the way to school, both of them thinking only of the dog.

CHAPTER 3

You have *got* to be kidding me!"

As Carly and Jimmy were opening their garage door to park their bikes after getting home from school, they heard a familiar voice that made them both freeze.

"Don't tell me you losers are my *neighbors!*"

Carly and Jimmy turned to see the blonde, freckled boy who had accosted them that morning standing at the edge of their driveway. His hands were resting on his hips, and his nose was wrinkled in a contemptuous sneer.

"Neighbors?" Jimmy asked, incredulous. The house on the right side of theirs was occupied by a kindly retired couple who often invited Jimmy and Carly in for hot chocolate. The house on the left . . . had been on the market for months.

21

The boy jerked his head in the direction of the house on the left. "Yeah. *Neigh*-bors," he said, overemphasizing the word for effect.

"Oh no," Carly muttered under her breath. Then, louder, she asked, "Did you just move in?"

"You guys really aren't the sharpest crayons in the box, are you?" The boy said. "Yeah. My mom and me just moved in last weekend."

Neither Carly nor Jimmy knew what to say to this. Okay, so they were neighbors. What did this boy *want*? Why didn't he just leave them alone?

Far from leaving them alone, the boy was striding up the driveway toward them.

"So did that dog die?" He asked.

Carly drew in her breath sharply and squared her shoulders. "*No*," she said as coldly as she could. "We didn't 'put the dog out of its misery.' You certainly have a short memory. Don't you remember that we decided to give the dog a chance to help the dog out? We decided to have the animal control specialist take the dog to the animal shelter, so the dog might be given a chance to live!"

The boy laughed. "So you mean it's going to die anyway?"

This time Jimmy interjected. "We're not going to let that happen," he said.

The boy shrugged. "Whatever, hero." The three of them stood looking at each other awkwardly for a moment, and then finally the boy spoke again. "Look, if you guys are going to be occupying my territory, you might as well know my name. I'm

Lonnie. And, like I said, this neighborhood is *my* territory—so stay out of my way."

Carly blinked. "Well. Lonnie. We've both lived here our whole lives. I don't know how moving in here last weekend makes this neighborhood your 'territory,' but maybe we should just agree to stay out of each other's way." She spoke in a clipped, stern voice.

Jimmy felt a rush of pride. Sometimes his big sister was so *awesome*.

Lonnie's face contorted into a scowl. He looked like he was about to make some smart remark, but just at that moment, a shining blue sedan pulled into the driveway and Carly and Jimmy's dad, whose name was Pete, emerged.

"Lonnie?" Their dad said before even greeting Carly and Jimmy. "Good to see you again, son. What are you doing in this neighborhood?"

Lonnie looked like he'd been socked in the stomach. "Mr. Endicott?" He stammered. "Do you *live* here?"

"Yes," Pete said. "These are my kids, Carly and Jimmy," he nodded warmly toward Carly and Jimmy, clearly oblivious to how tense the conversation had been before he arrived.

"Aw man, this is the *worst*!" Lonnie exclaimed. "Not only does my mom make me move to this nerd neighborhood, but now my ex-*principal* is my neighbor?" Without even pausing for a reply, he turned on his heel and stormed off in the direction of his house.

Pete sighed. He knew Lonnie well. Pete was the principal of another middle school, different from the one Carly and Jimmy attended. And he was, to his chagrin, all too familiar with Lonnie. At the end of the previous school year, when Lonnie was finishing seventh grade, he had been a regular visitor to Pete's office.

And these weren't friendly social calls. He had been sent there by his teachers for unending disciplinary issues: inability to pay attention in class, being disruptive, and even bullying other students.

Pete turned to his son and daughter. "So, Lonnie's our new neighbor, huh?" He asked wryly.

"That's one word for him," Carly said with uncharacteristic bitterness.

"Hey, Carly," Pete said gently. "Listen. Lonnie's had a tough time of it lately. His parents just got divorced at the end of last school year. I guess his mom decided to give him a fresh start in this school district."

Carly felt instantly guilty. She and her parents and brother had often talked about the fact that kids hardly ever misbehave in a vacuum. It was rare to meet a kid who was mean just for the sake of being mean. Usually, bullying was a sign that something else was going on.

"You don't have to be pals with him," Pete said, "but let's all do our best to be civil."

Carly nodded. "Okay, Dad. We'll do our best," she agreed.

Jimmy nodded solemnly too. Then the two kids turned to head into the house.

"Hold up a second, guys," Pete said. "Not so fast. I got a very surprising call this morning. Sounds like the two of you have something to discuss with me and Mom."

Jimmy and Carly exchanged a wary glance. They had known this was coming, but still they didn't feel prepared for it. They *hated* disappointing their parents. And they dreaded being in trouble. Were they going to have their privileges revoked? Maybe they wouldn't be allowed to go to the shelter to check on the dog. They both felt their hearts begin to thump ominously in their chests.

A moment later, Jimmy and Carly were gathered with their dad and their mom, whose name was Kim, around the kitchen table.

Kim folded her hands gravely on the table in front of her. She was a warm, fun-loving mother, and Jimmy and Carly rarely saw her truly mad. In fact, they felt like they'd lucked out with both of their parents. While most of their friends felt embarrassed or irritated by their parents half the time, Jimmy and Carly kind of enjoyed their parents' company. Of course, they wouldn't admit to it at school, but they really enjoyed regular board game nights with Mom and Dad and family trips to the amusement park or hiking in the gorges outside of town.

And they could always count on their parents to be fair about special requests, like when Carly wanted to go to a sleepover with her girlfriends or Jimmy wanted permission to spend his allowance on an MMORPG subscription. While it was their dad's job to keep middle school students in line and on track at school all day, he wasn't a hardliner at home. Sure, he let them know when they were out of bounds and both Carly and Jimmy had been grounded when they really deserved it. But they felt lucky that their parents were willing to talk things through with them and hear their side of the story.

So, seeing the disappointment on their parents' faces made their hearts sink. They stared down at the table, bracing for impact.

"We both got calls from your counselor at school this morning," Mom said. "It seems that you didn't show up for first period. And we had no idea what to tell them—last we knew was that you'd gotten on your bikes and headed off to school on time."

"We were absolutely terrified," Dad said. "We had *no idea* what could have happened. We were about to get into our cars and start scouring the neighborhood."

"We almost called the police!" Mom exclaimed. "So when I got a second call that you had both arrived at school safely, you can imagine how relieved I was. And then, how confused I was."

"What on earth happened?" Dad demanded. "Your counselor said you found a stray dog? What were you doing with a strange animal for over an hour?"

Carly put her forehead in her hands miserably. "I'm so sorry, Mom and Dad," she said. "We should have called you and explained right away. Jimmy even said we should have," she hurried on, not wanting to get Jimmy in trouble for something that wasn't his fault. "But I thought it was better to get to school as fast as we could."

"All right," Mom said, "slow down. Let's hear the whole story."

Carefully, Carly and Jimmy recounted the morning's events, finishing each other's sentences and trying to fill in every detail. By the time they had gotten to the end of the story, they had both forgotten that they might be in trouble and gotten caught up in concern for the dog all over again.

"So now, after all that, we don't even know what's going to happen to it!" Jimmy exclaimed. "Hank said the shelter might put it down!"

"All right, all right," Mom said, placing a gentle hand on Jimmy's forearm. "We're not angry with you," she reassured them both.

"In fact," Dad said, "I'm proud of you both. You showed compassion for a living being. That's exactly what your mom and I have raised you to do."

"You could have made different decisions along the way," Mom added. "You could have called your father and me, so that we could help you."

"Right," Dad said. "We might even have been able to come sit with the dog and wait for animal control so that you two could get to school. School always comes first."

"And so does honesty," Mom agreed. "Your father and I should have been part of the conversation from the beginning."

Carly and Jimmy nodded gravely.

"You're right," Carly said. "We're sorry."

"We're really sorry," Jimmy echoed. "We didn't mean to make you worry."

"It's okay," Mom said, forgiving them instantly. "We really are proud of you that you tried to help that dog."

"But that's just it!" Jimmy exclaimed, getting worked up all over again. "It might not be too late! We can still keep trying!"

Carly jumped in. "Right! Can we go to the shelter and see how the dog is doing? At least find out if it's going to be okay?"

"It's got a broken leg and maybe worse, and there's no one else to check on it and care whether it's going to make it or not," Jimmy pleaded.

Their parents exchanged one of those Mom-and-Dad-secret-language glances. In tense silence, Carly and Jimmy watched them communicate wordlessly with their eyes.

Finally, their dad let out a long sigh. "All right," he said. "Let's get in the car. We better get there before the shelter closes at six o'clock."

Carly and Jimmy almost yelped with relief.

A little over twenty minutes later, the whole family was standing in the small lobby of the county animal shelter, speaking to the shelter manager and the on-call veterinarian.

The vet's name was Dr. John Ancona.

"I wish I had better news for you," Dr. Ancona was saying. "Her right foreleg is shattered."

Jimmy raised his eyebrows. "Her?" He asked. "It's a girl?"

"Yup," Dr. Ancona said. "A strong female dog. Probably about two years old."

But Dr. Ancona went on, "The only way she could have sustained a break that bad is by being struck by a car. And that makes me worry that there might be further trauma."

"What does that mean?" Carly asked earnestly. "Further trauma?"

"Well, something like internal bleeding," Dr. Ancona said. "She's very weak. She clearly hasn't had any food in a few days, and she was malnourished even before she broke that chain and got away from whatever negligent owner she had.

So, she just doesn't have a lot of vitality built up to heal easily from the car strike."

Jimmy's face crumpled. Even though he was twelve years old, he felt himself leaning instinctively against his mother. Mom put an arm around his shoulder.

"So, what happens now?" Dad asked concernedly.

Dr. Ancona looked to the shelter manager with a grim expression.

"I'll be very frank with you," the manager, a kindly, round-faced woman named Eve said. "We have limited resources here that we have to funnel into animals that are adoptable. This dog needs surgery to reset the bone in her leg. She needs food to be reintroduced slowly, probably through a tube for a day or two. And from there, her prospects of becoming appropriately socialized are unpredictable. She had a bad puppyhood and has spent a lot of very scary days."

Eve paused, looking to Carly and Jimmy to make sure they understood the gravity of the situation she was describing. "When we take in an animal in this condition, the humane thing for us to do is to put it down before it has to suffer much more. Unless . . . well, unless there's a potential adopter willing to cover expenses and willing to commit to giving the dog a home once it's been treated."

Carly let out a yelp before she could stop herself. "But it has a *chance*! We could adopt it!" She exclaimed.

Dad placed a hand on Carly's shoulder.

"We talked about this possibility on the way over," he murmured to Jimmy and Carly. "The dog is suffering. It might be the kindest thing we could do to let it go."

Suddenly, Jimmy found that he was thinking clearly. The heaviness he had felt in his chest seemed to melt away. In that moment, all he wanted to do was to be heard.

"That's true, Dad," he said, "and if that really is the only option, then Carly and I will accept it. But I don't think it *is* the only option. If someone really pays attention to this dog, if someone cares for her, then she could get better. It's not fair not to give her a chance."

Jimmy could see that his parents were taken aback. Usually it was Carly who pushed back against them, and Jimmy who got too caught up in his emotions to express himself clearly.

"I think we should at least discuss the pros and cons," Jimmy continued matter-of-factly. "In fact . . ." he gave a dramatic pause. "I think it's time for Mom's whiteboard."

Despite herself and the tension in the room, Kim laughed. Her whiteboard was a bit of a bone of contention in the family. Kim had a very specialized job that her kids usually took zero interest in—before Carly and Jimmy were born, she had been what's called a "consultant," working with small business owners to help them measure and manage risk. She also taught one class at the local university to business students. In short, her class was about helping people answer one big question: How much risk is too much, in any situation? If you're trying to decide whether to start a business and possibly fail and lose all your money, how do you decide if it's worth it? When should you just not take the plunge?

After Carly and Jimmy came along, Kim had started teaching more and became a fulltime professor. But now that they were in middle school, she had gone back to a lot of her consulting work, advising businesses in town about risk management.

And that's where her whiteboard came in. Whenever the family had a high-stakes decision—when they really wanted a certain outcome, but just weren't sure if it was worth the risks involved—Mom brought out her whiteboard and walked them through the same Decision-Making Process she used with her clients.

Usually, the whiteboard made Carly and Jimmy and even Pete groan.

But not today.

"Seriously?" Mom asked. "You actually *want* to break this decision down with me?"

"I don't just want to," Jimmy said confidently, "I think we *have* to. That dog deserves a fair shot. And right now, all we have to go on are our feelings. Carly and I feel sorry for the dog and we want to protect her. You and Dad feel afraid that the dog is untrainable. We owe it to the dog to think more carefully about this."

Carly's face brightened. "Jimmy's right!" She exclaimed. "We don't have to just guess at an answer based on our fear and worry. We can talk this through."

Their parents exchanged that silent Mom-and-Dad look again. Finally, Mom turned to Carly and Jimmy with a smile on her face.

"All right," she said. "We'll go to the whiteboard. But let's all agree calmly that whatever decision we come to, we'll stick by it, even if it makes us sad."

Eve and Dr. Ancona were watching the family with bemused expressions.

"Well," Eve said, "I don't know what the whiteboard is all about. But it sounds like you're willing to consider adopting the dog?"

Dad gave a slow nod. "We're willing to *consider* it. But that's not at all a promise. And," he continued quickly, "we don't want the dog to hang in the balance suffering any longer than it has to. When do we need to come to a final decision?"

Dr. Ancona pursed his lips. "Good question," he said. "Frankly, if the four of you weren't standing here right now, I'd be putting this animal down tonight, before the shelter closes. As it stands, I can make it comfortable until tomorrow morning, but beyond that, I wouldn't consider it humane to delay surgery any further."

"We're not trying to rush this important decision or put pressure on you," Eve said, "but unfortunately, nature has its own timeline."

Mom and Dad nodded together.

"All right," Dad said. "Let's get home and have a family conference. And I'll call you first thing in the morning with our answer either way," he promised Eve.

"Wait," Eve said quickly. "Before you go, wouldn't you like to see the dog?"

"Yes!" Carly and Jimmy exclaimed in unison.

Eve brought the family through a heavy set of metal doors and led them down the center of long room bordered by kennels. As they passed, dogs leapt to their feet and pressed their snouts to their cage doors, barking and whining. A few cats stared nonchalantly at the passing family, and one stuck an orange-furred paw through the wires of its cage door and let out a friendly "Mraowr!"

Eve explained over the clamor of animal sounds, "We have a small, separate room for animals that are high-risk, so that they don't get stressed by being surrounded by so many other animals."

They passed through another set of double doors at the back of the room and found themselves standing in a small, dim room. In the corner was a large kennel, lined with blankets and towels. The dog was lying on its side, its eyes half closed, and its flank rising and falling steadily with its gentle breath. It did not lift its head when the family entered.

"I've sedated her," Dr. Ancona, who had come along, explained. "She was frightened and in a lot of pain. The sedative won't harm her; it will just make her much more comfortable and help her sleep through the night."

For the first time, Carly and Jimmy realized that the dog was beautiful. Dr. Ancona had cleaned her up a bit, and her charcoal fur shone in the dim light. Her muzzle was pointed, but not in a menacing shape—instead, Carly would call the curve of her snout graceful. She was very lean, but the strength of her sinewy body was clear. The creature looked noble lying there.

Jimmy turned to the rest of his family, drawing his shoulders back bravely. "We've got a lot to talk about," he said. "Let's do our best to be fair to her."

CHAPTER 4

Six steps of RISK MANAGEMENT—Step 1: IDENTIFICATION," Mom wrote with a flourish across the top of her whiteboard in the family living room. Then, she turned to face the rest of the family, a blue dry-erase marker in hand.

"We can actually use a step-by-step process to make this decision about the dog. The first step is the most obvious: we have to identify the problem and the possible courses of action."

Mom turned to Jimmy. "So," she asked, "what would you say the problem is, Jimmy?"

"The dog might die!" Jimmy blurted.

Carly sighed and rolled her eyes. "*You're* the one who said we didn't need to make this decision emotionally," she said, "and now you're getting emotional again."

Mom interjected before Carly and Jimmy could go off to the races bickering as usual.

"Well," she said in her measured voice, "Jimmy isn't exactly wrong. The dog getting euthanized is one possible outcome. But let's slow down. What is the question we are trying to answer?"

Carly sat up very straight, eager to be the perfect student as usual. "We're trying to decide whether or not to adopt the dog," she said.

"Right," Mom agreed, and scrawled, "Adopt dog—or not?" on the whiteboard.

"Now this is the part where we have to think a little bit more carefully," she said. "We have to focus on each possibility and walk through each one to determine its logical conclusion. That will help us brainstorm a list of possible outcomes."

"Kind of like a *Choose Your Own Adventure*?" Jimmy asked.

Dad, who had been listening quietly until now, smiled. "Yeah, it's a lot like that," he agreed. "Say you were trying to decide whether or not to do your homework. Option 1 is that you just don't do it. What's the most likely outcome of that course of action?"

"I'd get a zero on the assignment," Carly said. "And that would probably affect the rest of my grade, and maybe my privileges at school, too."

"Exactly," Dad said. "And what about Option 2? Say you do your homework? What are the pros and cons of that?"

"Well, if I do it," Carly said slowly, "I definitely won't get a zero. I don't know for sure what grade I would get. I think it would depend on how hard I work and how much I understand the assignment."

"Good!" Mom exclaimed. "So we can't predict the future with 100 percent accuracy. But, between Options 1 and 2, do you have enough information to choose the course of action that makes the most sense?"

"Of course," Jimmy said. "You do your homework."

"Right," Mom and Dad said in unison.

"But . . ." Mom added in a "Gotcha!" tone of voice. "Don't forget that if you spend the evening doing your homework, you won't be able to spend an hour texting with your friends, Carly. Or playing computer games, Jimmy. So there are still some consequences involved in choosing Option 2. Almost every decision has consequences. Let's call these consequences, or uncertainties, *risk*."

Carly nodded slowly. "Okay, I get it," she said. "So what are the possible outcomes in our situation with the dog?"

"Well, there are two major courses of action," Mom said. "Either we adopt the dog, or we don't. What are the likely outcomes if we don't adopt the dog?"

Jimmy groaned loudly. Carly put a hand on his knee and squeezed. "We're just talking it through," she reminded him quietly. Then, louder, to the rest of the family, she said, "The shelter will have to euthanize the dog if we don't adopt her."

Mom nodded. "That's the most likely outcome," she said, jotting notes on the whiteboard. "Is there any other possible outcome if we don't adopt?"

Jimmy thought for a minute. The exercise of thinking through the situation was helping him stay focused, rather than getting carried away by his concern.

"I honestly don't think there *are* any other possibilities," he said after a moment. "Dr. Ancona said that if we hadn't come to visit the dog, he probably would have put her down already. So, I don't think there's a risk that another family would come and adopt the dog before tomorrow morning, which is the deadline Dr. Ancona gave us. And, anyway, we're the only family that has a connection to the dog or cares about what happens to it. Any other family would have their pick of all the dogs in the whole shelter, and they probably wouldn't want a dog with a broken leg."

Dad nodded. "I have to agree with Jimmy. I think there's only one possible outcome if we don't adopt the dog."

"But, if we choose Option 2 and adopt," Mom said, "there are more possibilities—which means more uncertainty. Say we adopt the dog—what are some of the possible outcomes?"

Jimmy perked up. "We get a great new pet!"

Dad smiled wryly. "Sure," he said, "that's one possibility. Let's say the dog heals fine from its injuries and turns out to be perfectly friendly. A good family dog. There are still costs to the scenario. What are they?"

"We have to pay for the dog's surgery," Carly said.

"Yup," Dad said. "And we should get her spayed. And she'll need food and a leash and regular vet checkups. So there's a significant financial cost."

"And . . ." Mom added, her voice taking on an ominous timbre, "consequences associated with a particular decision don't just have to be financial. What other kinds of costs would be connected with getting a new dog?"

"Oh," Carly said, her face falling a little. "I get it. Time and, like, effort. We'd have to walk the dog every day—"

"Two or three times a day," Dad added.

"Right. And we'd spend time and effort feeding her and playing with her and giving her baths," Carly continued.

"And training her!" Jimmy said. "She probably needs a lot of attention because she's so scared and she hasn't had a good experience with people. So, we'd have to learn how to train a dog. Maybe even take her to classes?"

Mom was busily jotting all of this down on the whiteboard. Dad, meanwhile, was wearing his usual face of fatherly concern. "And those classes wouldn't be free," he murmured.

"Okay, slow down!" Mom called, barely able to keep up with them as she wrote down notes. "Let's pause on this, because to determine exactly how much the dog will cost financially, we'll probably have to do a little research. We'll also have to discuss who is going to take on the jobs of feeding and walking."

The whole family was silent for a moment. It was slowly starting to dawn on Carly and Jimmy that they were going to have to take more time to think through all of the possibilities and their consequences during this conversation. They exchanged a worried glance.

"And those are just the consequences associated with one possible outcome," Mom was continuing. "That's assuming the dog is relatively friendly and well behaved."

"Right," Carly said, a little sadness creeping into her voice. "The dog hasn't had a good life until now. So, we might not be able to train her. She might even turn out to be aggressive."

"Exactly," Mom said. "So now we're talking about all of the objective and subjective costs of owning a dog that we already listed, *plus* the cost of the time, stress, and anxiety of caring for a troubled dog."

"What would happen to her if we can't train her?" Jimmy asked, his voice catching a little in his throat.

Mom and Dad looked at each other. They were quiet for a moment, and Carly and Jimmy both understood from their silence that the answer was not a happy one.

Finally, Mom said, "Let's keep moving through the Decision-Making Process, and then we'll come back to that question."

They all turned to look at what Mom had written on the whiteboard so far. It looked like this:

Six steps of RISK MANAGEMENT
Step 1: IDENTIFICATION
PROBLEM: Adopt dog—or not?

OPTION 1:	OPTION 2:	
Don't adopt dog	**Adopt dog**	
POSSIBLE OUTCOME:	POSSIBLE OUTCOMES:	
Dog is euthanized	(1) Dog is a good pet	(2) Dog is untrainable
	COSTS:	COSTS:
	(1) Financial	(1) Financial
	(2) Time	(2) Time
	(3) Emotional investment	(3) Emotional investment
		(Stress and anxiety)

Suddenly, as he looked at the whiteboard, Jimmy felt a sinking in his stomach.

"Now I'm even more confused!" He exclaimed. "We have all these possibilities, and we have no idea what's going to happen! So how do we choose between them?"

"That's a really good question, actually," Mom said, her voice soothing and calm as usual. "This almost always happens with my students and clients. When you first start to break down a problem into its many parts, it might look even more complicated and difficult to understand than you originally thought. It's okay to feel overwhelmed at first. But we just have to keep going through the Decision-Making Process. You'll see. All of this will soon start to become clearer and a lot more manageable."

Carly wrinkled her nose. "To be honest," she said, "that's kind of hard to imagine."

Mom smiled patiently. "I'll show you," she said. "Let's move on to Step 2 in the Decision-Making Process."

Jimmy looked wary. "Okay," he said. "What happens now?"

"We've got to do our best to recognize the differences between the *subjective risks* and the *objective* ones," Mom said.

"I have no idea what that means," Jimmy said. Carly nodded her agreement.

"I'll explain," Mom said. "It's actually not hard to understand. *Subjective risk* is the type of risk we notice or observe based on our feelings and perceptions. *Objective risk* is the risk we can measure or quantify based on facts and data. It's easiest to understand if I give you an example."

She thought for a moment. "Say it's time for Carly to get her driver's license," she started.

Carly let out a whoop. "I want a convertible!" She exclaimed.

"Hold your horses," Dad said, laughing. "This is still *at least* three years in the future."

"So, we all know that there are risks involved with teenagers driving for the first time," Mom said. "When it comes time for Dad and I to decide when we're going to allow you to drive, and which car, and where you can drive it, we're going to have to evaluate the risks."

"Oh, I think I'm starting to see," Dad said. "So, as your parents, Mom and I are naturally going to be pretty worried about this big step. So we might *perceive* a lot of risk. We might worry that you'll get in an accident the first time you get in the car."

Mom nodded to show him he was on the right track.

"So, what we are describing is *subjective risk*," Dad continued. "But we should actually do some research, like looking at statistics that car insurance companies collect about teen driving habits. We could find out when and how teens are most likely to get into accidents, and what kinds of cars keep them safer if they do get into an accident. This would give us some indication of *objective risk*."

"So *subjective risk* is based upon your opinion and personal experiences, and *objective risk* is based upon facts and what can be determined with statistics and math?" Jimmy asked.

"That's a good way of thinking about it," Mom said.

"But how can you be sure of the difference?" Carly wanted to know.

"Aha," Mom said. "It's not always easy. Sometimes we take a detour. We often *think* that situations are more or less certain than they actually are based on how *familiar* we are with the situation and how much *control* we think we have over the situation.

"So," she continued, "if I take a particular risk every single day, I might underestimate how uncertain it actually is because I'm *familiar* with it. Also, if I think I have *control* over the outcome of a situation, I might think there is less risk involved in it than there actually is."

"Hey, that's pretty interesting," Dad said.

"I'm not sure if I get it," Carly said.

"Here's an example," Mom explained. "A lot of people are much more nervous about flying in an airplane than they are about driving in a car. This is because most people don't fly as often as they drive. So they're more *familiar* with driving. Also, when you fly, someone else is piloting the plane and responsible for your safety. When you drive yourself somewhere, you have a certain amount of *control*. So people believe flying is riskier than driving. That's their evaluation of *subjective risk*."

Mom paused dramatically. Carly leaned in, curious to hear what she was going to say.

"But guess what?" Mom said. "Statistics indicate for us that people are much more likely to be in a car accident than in a plane crash. Way, way, *way* more likely or probable. So, if we're talking about *objective risk*, traveling by car is much riskier than traveling by plane."

"Wow!" Carly said. "I didn't know that!"

"Now here's the other consideration," Mom continued. "I want to introduce you both to two new words that are important to understand when we are discussing decision-making. One is *frequency*, and the other is *severity*. With *frequency*, we are concerned with the number of times we observe an outcome during a specific time period. With *severity*, we are concerned with the size or magnitude of each observation that occurs. So, don't you think we should think about the *frequency* or *severity* of an observation or event? Isn't it possible that people might weight *severity more than frequency*, which might lead individuals to be less precise about risk? When an event is low-frequency and high-severity, our sense of *subjective risk* can be way off line as compared to what actually happened or was expected—*objective risk*."

"Huh?" Jimmy asked. "Low-frequency, high-severity?" "Yeah," Mom said. "Let's stick with the airplane example. It's actually really unlikely that a plane will crash. It's *low-frequency*, or *less likely to happen*. But if it *does* crash, the consequences are certainly very significant. It's *high-severity*. When people think about a *low-frequency, high-severity* event, they often think, 'It can't happen to me.' That's a subjective feeling; it's not objectively true."

"Oh," Jimmy said, nodding slowly.

"*Or*," Mom continued, "for some people, it's the reverse. If in the past you happened to experience or observe a *low-frequency, high-severity* event, you tend to overestimate the probability or likelihood that it will happen to you again."

"So how can we ever be certain that we're being objective and not subjective?" Jimmy asked.

"Well, we actually need to consider both," Mom said, "because we're trying to determine or forecast what might happen in the future, and we can almost never be 100 percent certain about the exact outcome. So it's always going to be somewhat subjective."

"But!" Dad exclaimed. "We can use research and critical thinking to get as close as we might expect to what actually occurs."

"Exactly," Mom said, obviously pleased to see that the family had understood the concept.

"So . . . let's get back to the dog," Carly said. "I think we need to do some research to help us evaluate the subjective risks and objective risks."

"That's exactly right," Mom said. "That's what Step 3 in the Decision-Making Process is all about: *analyzing and quantifying*. We need to get as much information and as many facts as we can to evaluate objective risks, and then we have to try to be honest with ourselves about which risks are subjective—which ones we just can't be sure about."

"So," Dad wondered, "maybe we try to estimate how much it will cost us to take care of the dog. That's definitely objective. And then we talk through the emotional ramifications if the dog turns out to be untrainable? That outcome would certainly be more subjective."

"I'd say that's a good place to start," Mom agreed.

Just then, Jimmy looked up. "Hey, where's Carly?" He asked.

"I'm a step ahead of you guys," Carly said, appearing in the doorway of the living room. She was holding their dad's iPad, which she had just run to his briefcase to retrieve. "Let's get researching!"

CHAPTER 5

Well, we've definitely got a lot to consider, kids," Dad was saying.

The sun had set a long time before. Carly and Jimmy's bedtime was fast approaching, and the family still wasn't sure what to do about the dog.

"Your dad's right," Mom agreed. "If we could say for sure that adopting this dog would be low cost and low risk, we'd get the dog in a heartbeat. As it stands, we're looking at a high cost/high risk situation."

She turned to look at the whiteboard. The family had tallied up the cost of adopting the dog: the adoption fee, the cost of the surgery, and the monthly price of food and toys and incidentals the dog might need. The total was well above Carly and Jimmy's combined allowance.

They had also listed the time and energy cost of caring for the dog, and the risk that the dog might not prove to be trainable after all.

But, there were also rewards involved in adopting the dog. Among the rewards that the family had brainstormed were:

- The opportunity for Carly and Jimmy to learn time management and responsibility by caring for a pet. (However, Mom had drawn a huge asterisk next to this point and added: *Provided that they uphold their end of the bargain.* She knew all-too-well that she was running the risk of having to pick up the slack if Carly and Jimmy failed to care for the dog as they had promised they would.)
- The potential emotional rewards of a lasting bond with a healthy, well-behaved, loving pet.
- Saving the dog's life.

These rewards that the family had come up with were more difficult to quantify than the financial cost of adopting the dog, but they were important to include as part of the decision.

"I have a question," Carly said. "If it's so clear that adopting the dog is high cost/high risk . . . why do I still *want* to get the dog?"

Mom gave one of her warm, understanding smiles. "Well," she said, "because logic isn't the only thing we use when we make decisions. We're human beings, so even if we've made a logical argument that makes sense to us *mentally*, we might still feel the complete opposite *emotionally*. These rewards are a major part of the equation, and they have to be weighed, even if we can't assign them a dollar figure."

She paused, considering, before she continued, "See, we're more than just our anatomy. We all have a soul or a conscience. And we all have *free will*—we can make our own decisions, and we have to bear the responsibility of those decisions.

"With that in mind," Mom went on, "let's move on to Step 4 of the Decision-Making Process. It's time to *rank* the possibilities we brainstormed in Step 1, using the *subjective risks* and *objective risks* we identified in Step 2 and the *analysis* we did in Step 3."

"What does that mean?" Asked Jimmy.

"I'll explain," Mom said. "We now have to weigh the possibilities against each other and decide which risks we're willing to tolerate and which ones we're not."

"How do we do that?" Carly wanted to know.

"You brought up a good point earlier," Mom said. "We know we're dealing with a high cost/high risk situation, but you still *feel* like you want to adopt the dog. That's because you would rather take on the risk of adopting the dog than the risk of *not* adopting the dog."

"But that's Carly's subjective feeling," Dad said quietly. "I've got to be honest with you, folks," he went on, "I'm just not convinced this is a good idea. I really value the order and structure of this household, and I'm not sure you two are aware of just how much having a dog will throw a lot of chaos into our home."

"It's true," Mom said ruefully. "And I have my concerns about whether you'll both stay committed—day in and day out—to taking care of the dog."

Jimmy nodded. "I know what you mean, Mom and Dad," he said. "I really understand that there are a lot of risks. But I think we can . . . what's the word, Mom?" He paused for a moment—then remembered. "We can *offset* those risks. Carly and I can promise to do the dog walking and training and feeding before and after school. And we can use our allowance to help pay for taking care of the dog."

"I think that's a very fair offer," Dad said. "Your allowance won't cover all the costs, but it would help you feel as financially invested in the process as Mom and I are. And I agree with your mom that the time and energy investment of training and taking care of the dog would be a good learning experience for both of you."

There was a brief silence, and then Carly spoke up, using her good-student voice. "For me, when I weigh the subjective and objective risks, I rank Option 2—*adopt the dog*—above Option 1—*don't adopt the dog*. I'd rather take on the risks associated with adopting the dog than the risk of the dog being euthanized."

"Me too!" Jimmy exclaimed. "My ranking is Option 2, then Option 1."

"Uh oh," Dad said. "I disagree. I'd rather *not* take on the risks associated with Option 2—*adopting the dog*. I rank them as Option 1, then Option 2." He turned to his wife. "What happens when there's a disagreement about how to rank options?"

Mom paused thoughtfully. Suddenly, her eyes brightened. "I think there's a compromise between Options 1 and 2 that we haven't considered!" She exclaimed. "I think there's a way to help us get more information about the risk that the dog might not be a good fit for our family."

Everyone looked at her in amazement.

"How?" Carly asked. "We can't predict how the dog is going to behave!"

"Nope," said Mom. "But we *could* get to know the dog better."

"Are you talking about some kind of trial period?" Dad asked.

"Exactly!" Mom said. "Right now, a big risk factor that we just can't measure is whether or not the dog is untrainable. And we've all agreed that if we *do* adopt the dog and realize we can't train her, we're in a bind. We didn't pursue that possibility all the way through to the end yet . . . but I think if that happens, we'd have to give her up, and that would be pretty devastating."

Jimmy looked at his hands, stricken. "That would be awful," he murmured.

"*But*," Mom said, "what if we take the dog for a 'trial period,' as Dad called it? We could give her enough time to get to know us, and us enough time to get to know her. Say . . . a month?"

To Carly and Jimmy's surprise, Dad was starting to crack a smile. It looked like he was persuaded by Mom's idea.

"That would also give Carly and Jimmy a real taste of what it's like to take care of the dog every day," he said slowly.

"What happens at the end of the trial period?" Carly asked.

"Good question," Mom said. "Let's slow down. Let's evaluate this option—let's call it *Option 3*—in the same way we evaluated Options 1 and 2, using the Decision-Making Process. What do we need to do in Step 1?" She asked the kids.

Carly spoke up right away. "Identify the possibilities!"

"Right!" Mom exclaimed. "There are two possibilities, as I see it. The first is that everything works out well: you and Jimmy do a good job caring for the dog, the dog responds to training, and we decide to keep her. The second possibility is that the dog doesn't adjust to our family. And in that case, I think we'd all need to do some research to find a no-kill animal shelter or rescue group that we could surrender her to, where we know she'd be safe and where there are staff members who know how to help animals with a bad history."

"Oh!" Jimmy gasped, his face brightening. "I didn't think of that! So there's another solution besides taking her back to the shelter to be put down."

"I didn't think of that either," Dad said. "It might be hard to find that kind of home for the dog, and we can't guarantee that they'd have space for her. But it is an option to fall back on."

"Now what about Step 2?" Mom said, before Carly and Jimmy could get carried away with their excitement. "We have to consider the subjective and objective factors. The dog does need surgery as soon as possible." She circled the price of the surgery that the family had put up on the whiteboard. "And there's also food and supplies for the month." She circled those figures on the whiteboard.

"Option 3 also has a risk that the other two options don't have," Carly said. "In a month, we'll get attached to the dog. So, if we have to surrender her, we're all going to feel pretty sad."

Mom nodded. "Would you call that a *subjective risk* or an *objective risk*?" She asked.

"It's subjective," Jimmy said, "but it's still real."

"It is," Mom agreed. "So it's part of making this decision." She turned back to the whiteboard. "We've pretty much already done Step 3—we've analyzed and quantified the costs. So, let's do Step 4—a new ranking of the options."

This time, without any discussion, the whole family agreed to rank Option 3 as the top course of action.

"So . . . what now?" Carly asked.

"Now, we move on to Step 5," Mom said. "We *make a choice . . . and we act on it.*"

Jimmy whooped. "We adopt the dog for a trial period!" He shouted, jumping off the couch and pumping a fist in the air.

Mom and Dad exchanged a smile.

"I think that's it," Dad said. "We've reached a decision."

Carly and Jimmy hugged each other, and then Carly rushed to the whiteboard and drew a big, blue circle around Option 3.

"Okay, guys," Mom said. "It's gotten really late. I think it's time for the two of you to go to bed—we're going to have a big day tomorrow bringing the dog home."

"Wait a second!" Jimmy said. "You said that the Decision-Making Process had *six* steps. We've only done five. What's Step 6?"

"Aha!" Mom said. "Great question. Step 6 happens after you make a decision. In Step 6, you *evaluate and adjust based on the outcomes.* Remember how we all agreed that we can't predict the future? Well, this dog is definitely going to surprise us in ways we couldn't predict tonight. So, as we go along, we're going to have to re-evaluate, and maybe change our plan. And we'll definitely have to revisit all six steps of the Decision-Making Process at the end of the month, when it's time to decide whether the dog stays with us. Can we all agree to do that?"

All four members of the family nodded. Then, Dad drew them all into a circle and put his hand into the center, palm down. Mom placed her hand on top of Dad's, then Carly put her hand on Mom's, and Jimmy stacked his hand on top of everyone's.

"Go team!" Dad shouted, and everyone cheered.

CHAPTER 6

Shouldn't we, like . . . *name* the dog?" Carly asked all of a sudden.

As soon as Carly and Jimmy got home from school the day after the family's whiteboard decision, they had all piled into Mom's SUV to pick up the dog. Dad had made the call to Eve and Dr. Ancona at the shelter earlier that morning to tell them that the family planned to adopt the dog on a contingency basis. Dr. Ancona had immediately prepped the dog for surgery on its broken foreleg, which had gone well.

Now the dog was in recovery at the animal hospital, and the family was on its way to pick her up—after having made a brief stop at the pet store to pick up a crate, food, and a few toys. Based on their whiteboard work from the night before, Carly and Jimmy had pitched in a percentage of their allowance, and Mom and Dad had covered the rest of the costs.

But all this time, they'd just been referring to the dog as . . . "the dog."

"How about Jimmy?" Jimmy asked.

Both he and Carly erupted into giggles.

"But she's a *girl!*" Carly exclaimed. "Besides, it'll drive you crazy every time you hear one of us say, 'Here, Jimmy!'"

"How about we name her Bernoulli," Mom said brightly, speaking over her shoulder to the kids in the backseat as she drove. "After the Swiss mathematician Daniel Bernoulli from the 1700s, who first started to talk about the concept of risk in terms of making decisions?"

Carly and Jimmy groaned.

"No way, Mom!" Jimmy said. "I don't even know how to *pronounce* that name!"

Mom laughed. "I'm just kidding. I'm glad you guys took enough interest in what I do to use the whiteboard yesterday. I won't push my luck."

"But wait a minute," Carly said, "I think Mom's onto something . . . The Decision-Making Process was such a big part of our choice to adopt the dog for a trial period. Maybe it could be part of her name somehow . . ."

"What do you mean?" Jimmy asked.

Carly was quiet, her mouth moving soundlessly. She was working something out in her head. Jimmy waited patiently; he knew better than to interrupt his sister when she was coming up with one of her bright ideas.

"I've got it!" She exclaimed at last. "Remember how Dad said last night that the dog will bring *chaos* into our ordered family life? Well . . . listen to this . . . The Decision-Making Process is all about making *Choices About Objective and Subjective risk*."

She paused and waited for them to figure it out.

"I don't get it," Dad said finally.

"*Choices About Objective and Subjective risk*," Carly said again, slowly, emphasizing the first sound of each word. "The first letters of each word spell . . ."

"Chaos!" Jimmy exclaimed.

"Exactly! Chaos! What if we call her Chaos?" Carly asked.

The car filled with a sense of wordless excitement.

"I love it!" Dad said. "Chaos the dog!"

"Chaos the dog, Chaos the dog!" Jimmy chanted.

"I'm really proud of you two," Mom chimed in. "You've already learned so much about making choices and weighing risks and rewards, just in the last day. I mean, think about it . . . You took a risk when you decided to be late to school and take care of that dog. Then your dad and I took a risk when we agreed to go to the animal shelter with you to visit the dog.

"We went into those risks a bit blindly," Mom continued, "but then we slowed down, and we took the time to evaluate the big decision of adopting the dog. And you've already come up with a cool way to remember what we've learned: *Choices About Objective and Subjective risk*—Chaos, our new dog! I think she's going to teach us all a lot about assessing and managing risk, which is a skill we can use in every part of our lives."

They drove on in happy anticipation, the whole car buzzing with eagerness to bring their new family member home.

＝ ＝ ＝

As soon as they walked into the recovery room at the animal hospital, Carly's jaw dropped open. The animal lying on a padded dog bed in the corner of the room was almost unrecognizable.

While she was sedated for surgery, Dr. Ancona's assistant had given her a bath. Even though Dr. Ancona had been able to clean her up a bit at the animal shelter, the dog had been too frightened for a really thorough cleaning. But now she was completely washed, so that the mats in her fur and the dried blood were gone.

The werewolf-like animal that had been hiding in the bushes had completely disappeared, and in her place was something more like an enormous teddy bear. With the mats washed and combed out of her fur, she was puffy and shiny. She was still the dark, charcoal color, but she looked soft, round, and huggable.

Dr. Ancona had shaved her right foreleg so that he could operate, and now it was wrapped in a white cast just like the cast Carly had worn after she broke her arm rollerblading. Every other inch of the dog was all soft, downy, slate-gray fuzz.

As Carly and Jimmy stared at her in amazement, Dr. Ancona explained, "Now that we've been able to get a good look at her, I'd say she's a pretty rare mixed breed. She definitely has some sheep dog in her—look at that puffy fur. But she's also pretty darn big. I'd guess there's some Tibetan mastiff in her, too."

"Wow!" Jimmy exclaimed. "Mastiff! That's so cool!"

"She almost looks like a Chow Chow," Carly giggled.

"She kind of does," the veterinarian's assistant agreed. "Maybe she's got a bit of Chow in her, too."

"Now," Dr. Ancona said, turning to Kim and Pete, "we think the four of you can handle Chaos—Carly and Jimmy are pretty grown up for their age. But let's talk about how to care for an animal with this dog's history."

Leaving Chaos to sleep in the recovery room, Dr. Ancona sat the family down in his office. He explained to them that the shelter staff was very careful about placing anxious animals in homes with children.

"We have every reason to believe Chaos will be a safe pet for your family, but we advise you to take it slow with her. Give her lots of space to adjust to her new environment. There's no need to rush anything. First just let her get used to your home and your presence, and as she starts to get more comfortable, you can think about doing more training."

Dr. Ancona gave the family some pamphlets about caring for an adopted dog, as well as some recommendations for obedience training classes.

And then—it was time to take Chaos home.

She was still snoozing when Dr. Ancona helped Kim and Pete get her inside her new crate. Then, it took the whole family to carry the heavy crate to the SUV and load it into the hatchback trunk.

The family spoke in soft murmurs as Mom drove them home, everyone being careful not to wake Chaos. Dr. Ancona had told them that though the surgery had gone very well, Chaos would be groggy for some time. They were supposed to let her sleep as much as she wanted to, and Dr. Ancona had also given them some pain killers to hide in Chaos's food so she would be comfortable as she healed.

As she drove, Mom explained in a low voice that decision-making has a long history—that it is in fact impossible to separate from human history itself.

"Early on in history," Mom said, "people didn't have numbers. Different civilizations had alphabets and written words long before they had symbols to represent numbers. This meant that their means of making precise calculations were limited.

"The first people to use numbers lived in what is now India and the Middle East. Once there was a common way of counting things that everyone could recognize, people were able to start making what's called *quantitative calculations*. Why do you think that was so important to our ability to make decisions?" She asked Carly and Jimmy.

Jimmy was thoughtful for a moment before taking a guess. "Well, when we were going through the Decision-Making Process last night, we needed to use numbers and calculations to talk about objective risk. Without a way to talk about exactly the cost of adopting Chaos, we wouldn't have been able to make a choice."

"Or," Carly added, "the choice we made would have been less informed."

"That's right," Mom agreed. "Once humans had numbers, they could look back at things that had happened in the past and start to establish patterns and trends. They could say, for example, 'Last year we grew *this much* wheat, and the year before we grew *this much*, so we can hope to grow *this much* this year.' This was the basis for the whole field of *statistics*."

"Like my baseball stats?" Jimmy asked.

"Right!" Mom said. "If you know a player has a certain batting average, that gives you a good foundation for predicting how he might perform in a future game. So statistics help us 'forecast' *possibilities*—things that might happen in the future. And they also help us think about *probabilities*—how likely a possibility is to occur."

"So, people didn't try to guess what would happen in the future before they had numbers?" Carly asked.

"Well, they probably did," Mom said, "but it was much more of a mystery. People thought of the future as being sort of off limits. When they talked about the future, they talked about it as being subject to the whims of their mythological gods. We know today that we can never be absolutely certain about the future, but we *can* use probabilities to make predictions about how the choices we make today might affect what happens tomorrow.

"This was really a breakthrough realization for ancient people. It opened up a whole new way of using logic and reason."

Carly and Jimmy listened carefully as their mother continued to explain the history of decision-making.

"Much later in history," Mom continued, "mathematicians came up with a way of drawing statistics visually—it's called a *bell curve* or *normal distribution*."

"Oh!" Carly exclaimed. "Like when we get graded on a curve?"

"Yes!" Mom agreed. "That's one way of using a *bell curve*. Basically, it's a way of showing which possibilities happen more frequently and which possibilities happen less frequently."

"I'll show you what it looks like," Dad said from the passenger seat. He pulled his iPad out of his briefcase and used the Paint app to draw a line that looked like the outline of a bell, like this:

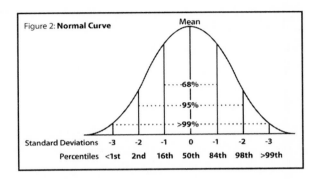

Figure 2: **Normal Curve**

"The top of the bell represents outcomes that happen very frequently," Dad explained. "So—in the example of grading on a curve—the top of the bell represents the grade that most students receive. The left bottom of the curve represents the very low grades, which happen infrequently, and the right bottom of the curve represents the very high grades, which also happen infrequently."

Carly and Jimmy passed the iPad back and forth, looking at the bell curve.

"So," Mom said, "if someone showed you a bell curve like this one representing a test that students took two weeks ago, could you use it to make a reasonably informed prediction about how students might do on the next test, two weeks from now?"

"Yes!" Carly said. "You definitely could."

"All of this boils down to what we call the *law of large numbers*," Mom said. "When you've done something a large number of times in the past, you can use the outcome that happened most frequently in the past to predict what is *likely* to happen in the future. But notice that I stress the word *likely*. As we've said before, we can never be sure about what is going to happen in the future. Exceptions to the rule happen all the time—there is always going to be that outlying instance of something happening that has absolutely no correlation to the past. That's what *risk* is all about. When something really good happens that we had no way of expecting or explaining, we call it a miracle. And when it's really bad . . . we call it a tragedy."

"The trouble is," Jimmy said, "even if the *law of large numbers* is a helpful tool, it still doesn't apply to Chaos."

"What do you mean?" Carly asked.

"Well, there's only one Chaos," Jimmy said. "We can't look back into the past and guess what will happen based on how other dogs have behaved because she is a unique dog with unique circumstances."

"Hey, you're exactly right," Mom told Jimmy. "Good work applying these principles to real life. In these circumstances, we have a lot of *uncertainty* and a lot of *risk*. Whether you call it uncertainty or risk, they both mean that we just don't know for sure what will happen. Something unpredictable could always occur, and take us by surprise."

"The important thing to remember about all of these concepts," Dad said, "is that the developments in human thought that your mom talked about really changed the way we make decisions—even in the face of risk and uncertainty.

Once people had these tools, they could start using analysis as an equal part of making decisions, right up there with their emotions—the subjective feelings that tug us in one direction or another. And once people started using both the subjective and objective together, we got a lot better at making choices."

"This is all pretty cool," Jimmy said. "It means that we don't have to worry so much about the future. It's not such a scary, unknown thing."

"Right," Mom said. "Of course there are always going to be things that are outside of our control. But if we think through questions we have about the future, we can start to feel better about taking risks—within reason."

"Which is exactly how I feel about adopting Chaos!" Carly exclaimed.

Just as she said this, the family arrived at their home, and Mom pulled the SUV into the driveway.

"Okay, remember what Dr. Ancona said," Dad said as all four of them worked together to carefully unload Chaos's crate—with Chaos inside—from the back of the SUV. "Chaos needs lots of sleep right now. Let's put her crate in the den and keep the lights low and the noise to a minimum. For the time being, while she gets used to her new environment, we'll keep her in the crate as much as possible, so she feels safe."

"That will make her feel safe?" Carly asked.

"Yup," Dad said. "Animals in the wild who are wounded go into their dens to heal. That's why you found Chaos hiding in the woods. Sometimes they actually *like* to feel like they're in a small, enclosed space where nothing dangerous can get to them.

"Once she's feeling better, she'll want to move around more," Dad continued, "When you get home from school tomorrow, she might be feeling more energetic, and we can try taking her out in the backyard together."

"Hey guys," a voice called from several yards away.

The family turned to see Lonnie standing in his front yard, watching them wide-eyed.

"What's in the crate?" He called.

Carly and Jimmy exchanged a brief glance. "Should we tell him?" Carly's eyes asked Jimmy.

Before they could decide, their dad answered. "Hey there, Lonnie," he said. "We've adopted a new dog."

Lonnie walked slowly towards them. His nose was wrinkled in distaste. From a safe distance, he peered through the wire door of the crate at Chaos's sleeping form.

"Wait a minute—" he said, his eyebrows shooting up in surprise. "Isn't that the creepy dog you two found yesterday?"

"Yes," Jimmy said tensely. "But she's not *creepy*. She's our dog. And her name is Chaos."

Lonnie snorted. He looked from Jimmy to Carly. "Wow," he muttered. "You guys are really crazy. Good luck."

He gave them a snide look, turned his back, and walked off toward his house.

CHAPTER 7

Where's Chaos?" Carly called the moment she and Jimmy arrived home from school the next afternoon. Carly and Jimmy had to stay after school for detention that day to make up for their unexcused absence from first period on the first day of school. But they hardly minded. They knew the punishment was fair—and they had used the time to get through most of their homework so that they could spend the evening with Chaos. As soon as they had parked their bikes in the garage and gone into the house, they were already calling for their parents.

"Mom?" Carly said again. "Where's Chaos?"

"Shhh," Carly and Jimmy's Mom replied, coming out of the living room where she had been reading. "Chaos is awake and out of her crate, but let's be very gentle with her. She's still getting used to us."

Mom brought Carly and Jimmy to the doorway of the den, and they all peered inside. Chaos was curled up at the foot of the couch. She lifted her head when she saw them appear and watched them wide-eyed, but she didn't make a sound. The raised fur, growls, and snaps that she had displayed when Carly and Jimmy first found her in the underbrush were gone. Now, she was quiet and watchful—not unfriendly, but a little on edge.

"I talked to Dr. Ancona a bit more this morning," Mom explained. "He gave me more information about how to get her used to people. She let me pet her—and I even put on her leash and took her out in the backyard for a bit this afternoon. But there are some rules to follow.

"For right now," Mom explained, "don't look her in the eyes. Animals look into each other's eyes as a sign of dominance, and so Chaos might see it as a threat. She hasn't growled at me all day, but if she *does* growl, that's her way of telling you she wants to be left alone. It doesn't necessarily mean she's going to try to attack, but it does mean she wants her space."

"Can we pet her?" Jimmy asked, looking carefully at the floor next to Chaos rather than straight at her.

"Yes, if she gives you permission," Mom said, "but let me tell you how to approach her first. Step 1 is to move very slowly when you're around her; if you rush towards her, she might think you're moving quickly to hurt her. Step 2 is not to move straight towards her. Approach her slowly from the side—again, it's less aggressive. And Step 3 is not to go all the way to her; stop halfway and crouch down, to make yourself smaller and less intimidating. Then it's up to her whether *she* wants to approach *you*."

Carly and Jimmy looked at each other, unsure if they were ready to give it a try.

"Why don't you go one at a time?" Mom asked. "That way she won't feel intimidated by all three of us at once."

"Okay," Carly murmured. "I'll go first."

Just as her mother had explained, Carly moved slowly into the den, careful not to move straight for Chaos, and looking off to the side of the dog. When she was about halfway into the room, she knelt down.

Chaos was lying on her side, her right foreleg, wrapped in its cast, outstretched in front of her. Sunlight was pouring through the windows at the back of the den, and shining over Chaos's soft, fluffy fur. She watched Carly curiously, and when Carly knelt down in the middle of the room, she thrust her snout cautiously forward and sniffed at the air between them.

"What now?" Carly said quietly over her shoulder to her mother.

"Well, Chaos might have had a bad owner before us," Mom said, "so Dr. Ancona told me about ways that we can reassure Chaos that we're going to be different—that we're going to be kind to her. If she was mistreated, we don't want to accidentally send signals that remind her of that scary behavior."

Carly and Jimmy both nodded, very serious.

"So, the first thing is not to reach too far out to her," Mom said. "Instead, let her decide to come to you. When you put your hand out, don't extend your arm all the way. Keep your hand close to you, and turn your palm up, so she can see that it's a friendly gesture and she won't misunderstand what you're going to do."

Carefully, Carly put out her hand, palm up, without reaching too far toward Chaos.

Again, Chaos sniffed the air cautiously. Then, slowly, she pushed herself to her feet. She had to lean on her left foreleg because even with the cast, she wasn't able to stand with weight on both front paws evenly. Slowly, almost comically, she limped over to Carly, keeping her snout low and sniffing as she went.

When she arrived in front of Carly, she sat down on her haunches and slowly moved her nose into Carly's open hand. She gave a few sniffs, then looked up at Carly expectantly.

Gently, slowly, Carly ran her hand over Chaos's shiny, dark head and down the side of her neck.

"Wow . . ." she breathed.

"Wow," Jimmy echoed. "Why is she so different, Mom? She seemed so scary when we found her, and now she's friendly!"

"Well, Dr. Ancona explained to me that when you first found Chaos, she was hurt, and so she was very vulnerable," Mom said. "But she didn't want you to *know* she was vulnerable and weak, in case you planned to hurt her. Animals don't have any way of knowing our intentions when they first meet us. So, she wanted you to think she was big and strong and mean as a way of protecting herself."

"Ohhh," Jimmy said, nodding. "Can I go pet her, too?"

"Of course," Mom agreed. "Just do the same things as Carly."

Jimmy moved slowly from the doorway into the den, stopping and kneeling several feet away from Carly and Chaos.

Just as Carly had done, he put his hand out, palm up, and waited patiently.

Chaos, who had been happily enjoying Carly's petting, noticed Jimmy. She sniffed the air in his direction, and then, with much less hesitation this time, hobbled over to him and allowed him to run his hands over her fur. A few moments later, Carly, Jimmy, and their mom were all seated on the floor with Chaos, happily petting her as she nuzzled their chins and blinked happily at them.

"Can we take her outside?" Jimmy asked.

"She's not ready to go on walks yet," Mom said. "She can't get far on the cast, but also she'd just be too spooked around all the smells and noise and cars and people. But I took her out in the backyard earlier today, and I think she'd like to go out again."

"I'll get the leash!" Jimmy said, jumping up.

Chaos jerked her head back when Jimmy moved suddenly. She gave a little whine and wobbled quickly to her feet, retreating toward the couch at the far end of the room.

"Jimmy!" Carly breathed, exasperated.

"Oh no," Jimmy said, his brow crinkling. "I'm sorry . . ."

"It's okay, Jimmy," Mom said gently. "We just have to develop new habits around Chaos. She's not used to us yet, and we aren't used to how quiet and still we have to be around her right now. Let's start over again. Try reintroducing yourself to her."

Jimmy went through the same steps all over again, approaching Chaos halfway and letting her come to him. It only took her a moment to "forgive" him for startling her. When she saw him put out his hand to her, she came gamely limping over on her cast and nuzzled his shoulder.

"Everything's okay!" Carly said, relieved.

"This is actually a good example of another aspect of risk management," Mom said, as she watched Jimmy and Carly petting Chaos. "There are two concepts that go hand in hand when we think about risk, but they're not quite the same thing: *peril* and *hazard*.

"A *peril* is anything that could cause a loss. For example, walking a tightrope is a *peril*; you could slip off and get hurt. And a *hazard* is anything that could increase the probability of that *peril* or loss happening. So, if the bolt that secures your tightrope isn't tightened properly, that's a *hazard*. It makes it more likely that the rope will come undone, causing you to fall."

Jimmy thought for a moment, patting Chaos's flank. "So the *peril* in adopting Chaos is that she might be unfriendly or might not get used to us . . ."

"And the *hazard*," Carly continued for him, "is how we treat her. Like, if we accidentally make mistakes that make her more nervous?"

"Yep, that's right," Mom said. "I think we probably *will* make mistakes because we're all new to this. But the fewer *hazards* we introduce into the situation, the less likely it'll be that we'll get into the *peril* of not being able to integrate Chaos into our family."

"So it's up to us to reduce the hazards . . ." Carly said.

"By changing our habits and following Dr. Ancona's instructions," Jimmy finished.

Carly smiled, then stood very gently, careful not to startle Chaos a second time.

"I'll go get her leash, and we'll take her outside," she said.

▬ ▬ ▬

Carly and Jimmy had been sitting in the grass in the backyard with Chaos for about a half hour when Lonnie appeared behind the hedge that separated his backyard from theirs.

"What are you weirdoes doing?" He called.

Carly and Jimmy exchanged a look and an exasperated eye roll. Jimmy stood slowly, having learned his lesson about sudden movements around Chaos. He started walking toward Lonnie, wanting to warn Lonnie about how important it was to be gentle and quiet around Chaos. But before he had gotten halfway there, Lonnie came through a gap in the hedge.

"What'd you name that dog again?" He said loudly. "Big Mistake?"

At the sound of Lonnie's voice, Chaos rose quickly and shakily to her feet, leaning heavily on her good, left foreleg. The hair on the back of her neck rose, and she put her head down and her ears back. She let out a low growl.

Lonnie sprang backward at the sight of her.

"Jeez!" He exclaimed.

His outburst only made Chaos more nervous. She growled again.

"Stop right there," Jimmy said sternly. Carly, who hadn't been quite sure what to do, was surprised and impressed at the authority in Jimmy's voice.

"You can't just come up to her like that," Jimmy told Lonnie, calmly but forcefully. "She's nervous, and she doesn't know you."

"That dog is dangerous!" Lonnie said, his voice still too loud. Chaos continued to growl.

"No. She's not," Jimmy said. "But she doesn't know you, and you're making her anxious. You have to follow certain instructions."

A look of frustration and pain passed across Lonnie's face. He took a slow step backward, away from Chaos, and then—to both Jimmy and Carly's surprise, he knelt down in the grass.

"I know what to do," he said softly.

As soon as Lonnie knelt down, Chaos seemed to grow a little calmer. The hair on the back of her neck settled. She took a few limping steps backward, putting Carly between herself and Lonnie, but she stopped growling.

Carly and Jimmy looked at Lonnie in amazement.

"I used to have a dog like her," Lonnie said, still speaking very quietly.

"What?" Carly and Jimmy said in the same instant. They were so surprised that they had forgotten themselves. At the sound of their voices, Chaos raised her head again and looked at each of them warily, but she didn't react further.

"Yeah," Lonnie said. "Well, he wasn't *my* dog. He was my dad's. I mean, not *was*. He probably still *is* my dad's dog. I don't really know—I don't go to my dad's house much these days."

Carly and Jimmy were both quiet, listening.

"Anyway," Lonnie continued, "it seems like Chaos is just like my dad's dog. She's nervous around strangers, sometimes acts a little mean? You have to approach her slow, show her your palm, let her get used to you?"

"Yeah . . ." Jimmy started, still somewhat stunned. "Yeah, that's right."

"I thought so," Lonnie said. "Rex—my dad's dog—is the same way. Dad got him as a rescue, so we don't know what happened to him, why he's like that. But he's scared of people at first. Just like . . . what's her name? Chaos?"

Carly nodded. "Yes," she said, "Chaos."

Jimmy was drawn into what Lonnie was saying. "So, did Rex get any better?"

"I mean; I guess it depends on how you measure 'better.'" Lonnie shrugged. "He never got comfortable with strangers. We couldn't really walk him in the neighborhood because there might be strange people or dogs, and we couldn't trust him to stay calm around them. But he got used to me and my mom, and he let us pet him and play with him."

Lonnie was quiet for a minute. "But he only really loved my dad," he said bitterly. A cloud seemed to pass across his face again, and his brow furrowed. "And the other way around, too. I think my dad loves that dumb old dog more than he loves me. If you ask me, those two deserve each other."

Lonnie stood up, keeping his head low and backing up slowly to show Chaos that he wasn't going to approach her.

"Are you leaving?" Jimmy asked. "Why don't you stay? We can introduce you to Chaos and see if she wants to be friends."

Carly sucked in her breath sharply. She didn't like that Jimmy had just made the decision on his own, without even checking in with her.

But she hadn't needed to worry. Clearly, Lonnie was not interested.

"Nah," he said. The sneer was gone from his voice, but he had returned to his usual standoffish posture. "You guys just got her. You probably want to play with her and get to know her by yourselves. Anyway, I have to help my mom with dinner."

Lonnie started to move back toward the hedge and his own house.

"Well," Jimmy said, "if you want to come play with her another time, you can. I mean"—he glanced at Carly— "you'd be welcome."

Carly didn't say anything, but she nodded.

"Okay," Lonnie said. "Just . . ." He seemed to be struggling to find the words. "Just . . . be careful, you guys. Having a dog is harder than you think."

Before Jimmy or Carly could ask him what he meant, he had ducked back through the hedge and was gone.

CHAPTER 8

That night at dinner, Carly told her parents what had happened with Lonnie, and Jimmy occasionally interrupted to fill in details.

"So we have no idea what he even meant!" Carly finished. "He just told us to be careful."

Carly and Jimmy's dad sighed. "Listen, guys," he said to them. "Lonnie's had a pretty rough time, even before his parents got divorced."

"Yeah," Carly said, quietly. "He kind of hinted that he and his dad don't get along well. I feel bad that we haven't been nicer to him."

"Well, we *did* tell him he could come over and get to know Chaos if he wanted to," Jimmy interjected.

"That's true," Carly said. "Or, actually, *you* told him that. I don't know if I would have let you if you'd asked me first. But I'm glad you did now. Maybe he just needs people to give him more of a chance."

"I think that's probably true," Dad agreed. "But like I said before, I'm not going to make you be friends with him. You don't have to hang out with him if you don't want to, but I do want you to try to be understanding of him. He's dealt with a lot of things that you and most of your friends haven't had to face."

Both Carly and Jimmy nodded their agreement.

"We definitely will, Dad," Carly said. "You know, Lonnie said something that made me feel awful. He said, 'My dad loves his dumb old dog more than me.'"

Mom gave a low hum of sympathy in the back of her throat. "It's too bad that he feels that way," she said.

"It is," Dad agreed. "I doubt it's true, but it must have been hard for Lonnie if he felt like he couldn't get the attention he needed from his dad. And that might give us a clue about why he acted so harshly when you two found Chaos—and again when he found out we had decided to adopt her. He might just not like dogs very much because of how his dad was with Rex."

"Wow," Carly said softly. "I never would have thought of that. I guess there's so much more going on for people when they act mean than we can ever know."

"You're right," Dad said, "which is why I'm encouraging you and Jimmy to give Lonnie a chance. He's not a bad kid—but he's got a lot of reasons to act defensively and to try to push people away."

"Maybe we *should* try to be friends with him," Carly said. "Maybe if he had the chance to feel accepted, he wouldn't be so defensive. And he might even get into less trouble."

"Right!" Jimmy agreed. "And maybe getting to know Chaos better could even help him get over his bad experience with Rex."

Mom nodded slowly. "Maybe," she said. "And I think it's really great that the two of you want to help Lonnie if you can."

"But remember," Dad added, "Lonnie's a human being, not a project. He's got his own ideas and hopes and plans—and they might be compatible with yours, but they also might not be."

"I think your dad is actually expressing an idea that fits into what we've been learning about making decisions," Mom said. "It's the concept of *free will*."

"Oh yeah," Carly said, remembering. "Didn't we talk about that a little when we were making our whiteboard decision about Chaos?"

"Yes," Mom said, "we certainly did. Free will is a gift all human beings have—and it's a responsibility. As human beings, we have intelligence and the capacity to envision what the future might be like and to imagine what it's like to be in someone else's shoes. That means that when we make decisions, we have a pretty big responsibility. We have to consider more than just our own desires; we also have to consider *who we're called to be* as human beings. We have to think about how our choices might affect other people and shape the future."

"Your mom brings up an interesting idea," Dad said. "Remember how, when we were making the decision about Chaos, there was a point where it seemed like logic (the Six

Steps of Risk Management) and your emotions (what you *wanted* to do) just weren't matching up?"

"Yeah," Jimmy said, "I remember that. It seemed like it was too much of a risk to adopt Chaos, but Carly and I still *wanted* to."

"Well," Dad continued, "we went through a process of critical thinking, and that critical thinking led to the action we ultimately decided to take—we adopted Chaos for a trial period. It could just as well have led to our *in*action—we could have decided *not* to adopt Chaos. And in turn, our actions or our inaction determines our results in life. So, in a very real way, our critical thinking shapes our lives."

"Right," Mom agreed, "but everyone's critical thinking has an origin—it has a basis in something. Our subjective and objective considerations are shaped by who we are: where we come from, our relationships with our families, the values our families have taught us, and the experiences we've shared with them, and so on. These influences all come together to create a sort of 'subjective and objective compass' for us that helps steer us when we're thinking critically and making decisions."

"Wait a minute, I think I get it," Jimmy said. "So, my 'compass' was telling me that adopting Chaos was the right thing to do—and that came from the values you and Dad have taught me?"

"Exactly!" Mom and Dad agreed at the same time.

"And," Mom continued, "your compass can change as you go through life. Your critical thinking, plus the actions you do or do not take, plus the outcomes or results of those actions all add up to the path of your life. So it's up to you whether you keep stretching your thinking beyond its limits and keep growing, *or* . . . whether you just stick with the status quo."

"What's the *status quo*?" Jimmy asked.

"It means 'the way things have always been,'" Carly jumped in.

"That's right," Mom said, smiling. "If we don't recognize that we have free will and that we are actively steering ourselves through life with each decision that we make, then we risk just floating through life randomly, making decisions based on how we feel in the moment without any foresight or critical thinking. If we do that, we'll always be stuck in the status quo instead of actively and purposefully growing."

Dad was nodding thoughtfully. "We talked about how critical thinking and using the Decision-Making Process can help us when we face *uncertainty* about the future. But it can also help us when we face *temptations*—things that might seem like a reward in the short-term, but aren't so good for us in the long-term, or aren't so good for the people around us."

Dad took a sip of water before continuing to speak. "I think that's a pattern Lonnie has gotten stuck in. He chooses what makes him feel good in the moment instead of thinking more critically about his decisions. And that's why he often gets into trouble."

Mom leaned back in her chair, continuing Dad's thought. "Now that the two of you know about the Six Steps of Risk Management," she said, "you have an alternative. Instead of just reacting based on your desires and what you want in the moment, you can rely on your internal compass and your critical thinking to guide you to actions that take the future and other people into account."

"You know, one of my students went to West Point after he graduated from high school," Dad said, "and he sent me an email telling me how he was doing there. He mentioned that the cadets at West Point have a prayer, and one of the things they ask for in that prayer is: '*Make us to choose the harder right instead of the easier wrong.*'"

Carly and Jimmy had finished their dinners, and now they began to help clear the plates from the table. As she gathered up the silverware, Carly said, "Well, it seems like being friends with Lonnie would be the 'harder right.'"

"I think so, too," Jimmy agreed. "But, hey! Maybe we can use the whiteboard to help us decide what to do."

Mom's eyebrows sprang up. "Are you saying you actually *want* to use the whiteboard?" She asked in joking astonishment.

"I think it's a great idea!" Carly exclaimed.

She and Jimmy quickly washed the dishes and cleaned up the kitchen, and then they all gathered around the whiteboard in the living room. Chaos had been resting in her crate through dinner—she seemed pretty worn out from her afternoon of getting used to all four members of the family—but they all carried the crate into the living room so that they could keep her company as she dozed.

This time, Jimmy took charge of the dry-erase marker.

"So, Step 1 is identification," Jimmy said. "What's the problem and what are the possibilities?"

"Easy!" Carly said. "The question is: Should we be friends with Lonnie? And the possibilities are . . . we either try to make friends with him, or we try to stay away from him as much as possible."

Jimmy jotted these things down on the board.

"Step 2," he said, "is to consider the subjective and objective risks."

"Hmm," Carly said, "that's trickier. Aren't the risks mostly subjective? Since Lonnie is a person and we don't *know* how he's going to behave? We can't measure or quantify his behavior."

"That's true," Dad said. "In this case you know a few objective facts about Lonnie—who he is, a little about what has happened to him in the last year, and a bit about how he has behaved in the past."

Mom nodded. "But mostly you have to factor in the subjective risk of how he might treat you if you become friends with him."

"I guess the risk is that he ends up being unkind to us and not the kind of person we want to be friends with," Carly said.

"Right," Mom agreed. "So, is there any risk to the other possibility you identified in Step 1? In other words, is there any risk to inaction—*not* becoming friends with him?"

"I think so," Jimmy said. "I think we risk being unkind ourselves."

Everyone in the room suddenly got very quiet as they considered what Jimmy had just said.

"That's very true, Jimmy," Mom said. "There's no measurable loss to you in terms of money or time or effort . . . but there is still a serious risk in terms of how you think of yourselves and the people you want to be."

As Jimmy jotted this "risk" down on the whiteboard, Carly was already ready to move on to Step 3.

"Wait a minute," she said, "the risks we've identified are pretty subjective, so how can we do Step 3—analyze and quantify? Like you said, Mom, we can't really measure these risks in any objective way."

"Right again," Mom said. "Sometimes, when we're going through the Decision-Making Process, we hit the limits of logic and reason. Where logic and reason run out, we sometimes have to just take a *leap of faith*. We have to trust our internal compasses to steer us in the right direction."

"Well," Jimmy said, "in Step 4, we rank the possibilities. And my internal compass is telling me that I'd rather try to be friends with Lonnie than not."

"Me too!" Carly said.

"That was easy," Dad said with a smile. "It sounds like you guys are already at Step 5—make a choice."

"Wait . . ." Jimmy said, pausing. "If our choice is to be friends with Lonnie . . . how do we do that?"

Mom laughed. "Well, guess what?" She said. "Lonnie has just as much free will as either of you do. So, you can extend an olive branch—but he gets to decide whether or not to accept it. And you have to accept his decision."

"I think we should invite him to join us and play with Chaos the next time we see him," Carly said.

Jimmy nodded his agreement. "Deal," he said.

Just at that moment, Chaos lifted her head and gave a long, satisfied yawn.

CHAPTER 9

Chaos let out a mournful yowl and sat back on her haunches, pulling against her leash. Her ears were flat against her head and she was trembling slightly.

"Come on, Chaos," Jimmy said gently, holding the leash firmly but not pulling back against Chaos. "We're just going to go one time around the block."

She yowled pitifully again.

"Just five minutes," Jimmy pleaded. "Come on, Chaos, just one time around the block."

Carly, who was standing beside Chaos and gently stroking her fur, sighed forlornly.

"It's never going to work, Jimmy. We're *never* going to get her to take a walk."

It had been almost two weeks since Chaos had come to live with Carly and Jimmy and their parents. Her leg was healing well—it would still be in its cast for several more weeks, but she could hobble along fairly well. She had gotten used to the family home and backyard and now had the run of the place. She was comfortable sleeping outside of her crate and was happy to go out into the backyard with Carly and Jimmy twice every single day.

But taking a walk was a different story.

Even though the speed limit in the neighborhood was only twenty miles-per-hour, and all the passing cars tended to respect it, Chaos was *terrified* of any vehicle that went by. If she heard a car approaching, she would immediately cower, belly to the sidewalk, and flatten her ears against her head, whimpering.

Passing pedestrians were just as much of a problem. Chaos never got aggressive—the aggression Carly and Jimmy had witnessed when they first found her seemed to be a passing symptom of her fear and injury. But she didn't want anything to do with any human being who wasn't a member of her family. If she saw a person—especially an adult—approaching, she would immediately retreat behind Carly or Jimmy and growl plaintively.

Because of these anxieties, it had been pretty much impossible to take Chaos out anywhere but the family's backyard. All the same, Carly and Jimmy tried every day to get Chaos to walk with them around the block. Dr. Ancona had advised them that the sooner they could prove to Chaos that the neighborhood was safe, the easier socializing her would become. If they didn't expose her to the outside world, her fears would only grow.

So, every day, the siblings put on Chaos' leash and brought her out the front door to the sidewalk that looped around the family's cul-de-sac. They usually never got much farther than twenty yards away from the house before Chaos sat back on her haunches—as she was doing now—and flat out refused to budge another inch. Then, out of pity for her, Jimmy and Carly would concede and take her to the backyard instead.

If a car happened to pass as they were coming outside, all bets were off. Then, instead of just sitting back and refusing to walk, Chaos would yowl so loudly and miserably that Jimmy and Carly were afraid the neighbors would think she was hurt. And so, to the backyard they would go, defeated again.

Today, in the mid-morning on a Saturday, the street was relatively quiet. There were no passing cars and not a pedestrian in sight.

Or so they thought.

From behind them, they heard a soft voice call, "Hey, guys."

Carly and Jimmy turned to see Lonnie on the sidewalk several yards away, standing astride his bike. As soon as she heard his voice, Chaos whimpered and lay flat on the sidewalk.

It had been a while since Carly and Jimmy had seen Lonnie—in fact, they hadn't seen him around the neighborhood since they had made their whiteboard decision to try to befriend him. They hadn't seen him at school either; he was a year ahead of Jimmy, and even though he was in the same grade as Carly, they didn't happen to share any classes.

But, clearly, Lonnie remembered what he had learned about Chaos. He got off his bike and quietly put down its kickstand. Then he approached slowly, and when he was several yards away from Carly, Jimmy, and Chaos, he knelt down to make himself smaller and less threatening.

Chaos was clearly intrigued, but still nervous. She didn't advance toward Lonnie, but she did cock her head and look quizzically at him.

"It might calm her down if one of you comes over here," Lonnie said softly. "It doesn't always work, but if she sees that you trust me, sometimes that helps a dog to understand that a person isn't dangerous."

Jimmy smiled. It was a good idea. He gave Chaos a reassuring pat, handed her leash to Carly, and then moved over to where Lonnie was waiting. He knelt down next to Lonnie, and—slowly, so that he wouldn't startle Chaos—he slung an arm around Lonnie's shoulders.

For a moment, Lonnie froze. It seemed like he was almost more surprised and anxious than Chaos. Both he and Jimmy turned and looked to Chaos to see how she would react. Her flattened ears had lifted away from her scalp and she was watching them attentively. She had stopped the whining and growling noises in the back of her throat.

After a breath, Lonnie relaxed.

"Hey, man," he said to Jimmy, still keeping his voice low to avoid scaring Chaos. Then he turned to Carly and said, a little louder, "Hi, Carly."

"Hi," Carly called back, smiling.

She took a few steps toward Lonnie and her brother, making sure to keep the leash somewhat slack so that Chaos knew it was up to her whether she wanted to follow or not.

A moment later, to all of their surprise, Chaos had risen from the sidewalk and was loping along behind Carly, limping charmingly on her broken leg. When they arrived near the two boys, Chaos stuck out her snout and sniffed the air in their direction.

Lonnie gently stretched out a hand toward Chaos, palm up. She gave him another sniff, then sat down and eyed everyone calmly, as if to ask, "What's the big deal, guys? What are you making all this fuss about?"

Lonnie chuckled. "I guess it worked," he said.

"Yeah," Jimmy said, pleased. "She seems to think you're all right."

"Maybe she smells Rex," Lonnie said.

Carly and Jimmy were a little surprised. From the way Lonnie had talked last time, they hadn't thought he ever saw his dad and Rex anymore.

Lonnie registered the curiosity on their faces. "I've been at my dad's place this week," he explained. "Just came home this morning. My grandparents were in town visiting my dad, so my mom said it was okay for me to go."

Neither Carly nor Jimmy was entirely sure what Lonnie meant by this, but they wanted to keep the conversation going, to let Lonnie know that they were on his side and interested in how he was doing.

"When was the last time you saw Rex?" Carly asked.

"It's been a couple months. I didn't go to my dad's house all summer," Lonnie said. Chaos, who had relaxed completely, was allowing Lonnie to pet her, and running his hand over her smooth fur seemed to be calming him down just as much as it was her.

"How's Rex doing?" Jimmy asked, trying to keep things light and friendly.

Lonnie grinned. "He's actually doing pretty good. My dad's house was full of people—me and my grandparents *and* Dad—and Rex still did all right. He's still not up for taking walks, but he didn't get aggressive with anyone. And I think he's getting more accepting of me."

Then, the cloud returned to his face and his brow furrowed. "But it's still annoying how much my dad loves that stupid dog. It's like—there are other people in his family. My grandparents and I were there *all week* and he hardly paid attention to any of us."

"I'm sorry, Lonnie," Carly said sympathetically.

"Yeah," Jimmy said, "that sounds really hard."

Lonnie looked at them and blinked. It seemed to take him a moment to realize that they weren't making fun of him. Then his face softened. He looked away and shrugged, seeming to get embarrassed that he had allowed himself to say so much in front of them.

"Whatever," he said. "It's no big deal. It's not like I care, anyway."

The three of them were quiet for a moment, and Lonnie continued to gently pet Chaos.

"Are you trying to get her to walk around the neighborhood?" Lonnie asked finally.

"Yeah," Jimmy said, "but we haven't had much luck. She's too scared to go far from the house, and if a car passes by—it's all over."

"Have you tried positive reinforcement?" Lonnie asked.

"What's that?" Carly asked.

Lonnie snorted. A little of his arrogant side was creeping back.

"How do you expect to train her if you don't know what positive reinforcement is?" He asked. "It's so basic."

"Well," Jimmy said patiently, "why don't you show us?"

Lonnie looked a little confused for a second. It was almost as if he had been trying to start a disagreement—*trying* to get Carly and Jimmy to reject him—and it hadn't worked.

"Uhm," Lonnie stammered, "okay." He paused, unsure where to begin. "Well," he said finally, "it's actually pretty simple. It's this idea that animals are like people. They respond more to being rewarded than punished. So, instead of punishing dogs when they do the things you *don't* want them to do, you reward them when they do the things you *do* want them to do. They start to associate the good behavior with the positive reward, and then they're more likely to behave the way you want."

"Cool," Jimmy said. "That sounds easy. What kind of rewards do you use?"

"It can be as simple as verbal praise," Lonnie said. "Or . . . is she food motivated?"

"Food motivated?" Carly asked.

"Yeah," Lonnie said. "Like, does she get really excited when it's time for her to eat?"

Carly and Jimmy both laughed. "Uh, *yeah*!" They both said in unison.

"Then we could try that now," Lonnie said. "Do you have any treats for her?"

"We have some inside, in the kitchen," Carly said.

Lonnie gave an exasperated sigh, as if he were dealing with two dimwits. "You didn't bring her treats with you? How do you ever expect to train her?"

Carly grinned and shrugged. "Well, now that we know they're important, we won't forget again. Thanks, Lonnie!" Again, Lonnie looked a little astonished. It took him a moment to realize Carly wasn't being sarcastic. But by that time, she had already rushed back to the house to retrieve the treats.

When Carly returned with a packet of bite-sized dog biscuits in hand, Lonnie explained more about positive reinforcement.

"You just want to see if you can get her to take baby steps toward the behavior you want," he said. "So, instead of trying to get her to go all the way around the block, which is actually pretty far from home and probably pretty scary for her right now, let's just see if we can get her to go a few steps down the sidewalk."

"Okay," Jimmy and Carly agreed.

Lonnie took the treats from Carly and put one in his palm. He held it out to Chaos just far enough so that she could smell and see what he was holding in his hand. Immediately, her ears perked up and she sniffed toward his hand excitedly. But before she could rear up and shove her snout at his palm, Lonnie began to back slowly away from her.

It seemed like Chaos didn't even realize what was happening. She was so focused on following the treat in Lonnie's hand that she walked after him a dozen yards down the sidewalk. Eventually, Lonnie stopped, gave her an enormous, "Good girl!" and handed her the treat. As she chomped away happily, he rubbed her ears and the sides of her neck.

"Wow!" Carly and Jimmy caught up to them. "It worked!"

"Should we go further?" Jimmy asked.

"You know," Lonnie said, "I'd actually say not today. Look, she's already starting to realize how far we've gone." Sure enough, Chaos had finished her treat and was scanning the unfamiliar bushes and grass around them nervously.

"Also," Lonnie said, "you can only give her so many treats in a session before she gets tired of them. And then they won't be as reinforcing. I'd say let's walk her back to your backyard. That will actually show her that you're not going to push her too far. The easier each little step you take with her is for her, the more progress she'll make."

"Huh," Carly said, "that's amazing. I don't think we ever would have thought of doing it that way."

"I mean, it takes a lot of patience," Lonnie said, as the three of them walked around the side of Carly and Jimmy's house with Chaos limping beside them. Now that they were approaching more familiar territory, she seemed to be completely at ease. They opened the gate and passed into the backyard.

As they walked, Lonnie continued, "For whatever reason, my dad has patience in spades when it comes to Rex. But not for me."

Carly and Jimmy were both quiet, deciding to let Lonnie take his time and reveal what he wanted.

"My dad has a drinking problem," Lonnie said suddenly, in a rush, as if he were afraid that he wouldn't be able to get it out if he didn't blurt it at top speed. "So that's why I don't see him much anymore. He's not a mean drunk or anything. He's just irresponsible—that's what Mom calls it anyway. But he seems to do fine with Rex. Just not with me. The only reason my mom let me go over there this week is that my grandparents were around too."

"Wow, Lonnie," Carly said softly, "I'm really sorry."

"It's not your fault," Jimmy said. "I'm sure your dad cares about you a lot."

Lonnie shrugged and looked at the grass. "I doubt it," he muttered.

Then he looked up and gave Chaos a friendly pat. "Anyway, whatever," he said, clearly not wanting to continue that line of conversation. "Chaos is pretty cool. She's a lot sweeter than Rex anyway. I'm sorry I was such a jerk about her in the beginning. And, uh . . ." he trailed off for a moment, then picked up steam again. "Sorry I was a jerk to you guys."

Carly and Jimmy both smiled and shrugged in the same moment.

"It's okay," Jimmy said. "Thanks for helping us with Chaos today. You really made a big difference."

Lonnie smiled back. "I wasn't convinced at first. I thought you guys were just going to get attached to her and you wouldn't get anything out of it. It would just be a total loss. But I think I was thinking too much about Rex and not thinking about how Chaos is her own dog."

Carly nodded. "That's what we're learning, too. There are some things you just can't predict about dogs—and people. So you have to take a leap of faith."

"A leap of faith," Lonnie repeated. "I like how that sounds."

CHAPTER 10

"Good girl, Chaos!" Jimmy and Carly exclaimed. Carly handed Chaos a treat as Jimmy showered her with praise and gave her a generous rub around her head and shoulders. Their parents were watching from the front doorway with broad grins spread across their faces.

Chaos had just walked around the entire block.

Not only that, but they had passed the Farber twins, who were six years old, playing on their Big Wheels in their driveway, and she hadn't growled at them. They had also passed Mrs. Russell walking her Pomeranian, and while Chaos had hung back behind Jimmy and Carly as they walked by, she hadn't barked, snapped, or strained against her leash. And the kicker: at least three cars had driven by during their walk without incident. Chaos had flattened her ears, ducked her head, and waited stoically for the cars to pass. Once they were gone, she proudly lifted her head high and continued to limp forward gamely.

Lonnie had been out riding his bike and had joined them for the second half of the circle around the block. Now, he gave Jimmy and Carly both a high five.

"I *knew* she could do it if we all stayed patient!" He exclaimed. Almost as if she understood him, Chaos butted her head against his leg. He gave her a scratch behind the years.

"I actually promised my mom I'd help her clean the garage tonight," Lonnie said, "so I'll see you guys later." He lifted his hand and waved to Kim and Pete in the doorway. "Have a good evening, Mr. and Mrs. Endicott!" He called. Then, he jogged off toward his house.

As Carly and Jimmy came inside and began to unclip Chaos from her leash, their mom smiled brightly.

"It seems like Lonnie is really warming up to you guys, huh?" She asked.

"Yeah!" Jimmy said. In fact, the transformation had been quick and amazing. Lonnie had joined Carly and Jimmy for many of their training sessions with Chaos. He had a huge hand in gently, incrementally getting her to move further and further from Carly and Jimmy's front yard. And the more success they had with Chaos, the warmer Lonnie got.

It seemed that what Carly and Jimmy's dad had told them was right: Lonnie just needed to be given a chance. He wasn't used to people being kind to him, so he acted mean first as a kind of defense mechanism. But once he saw that Carly and Jimmy *wanted* to be friends with him, he was eager to reciprocate.

He had invited Jimmy over several times to play computer games with him. He'd invited Carly, too—but it just wasn't really her thing. So, instead, when the three of them wanted to hang out, they took their bikes around the neighborhood together or jumped on the trampoline Lonnie's mom had set up in their backyard.

Carly and Jimmy were quickly starting to think of Lonnie as one of their best friends. After all, they never would have gotten so far with Chaos without him. And, by this time, Chaos meant the world to them.

"Hey guys," Dad said as Carly and Jimmy were pulling off their shoes and settling in for a quiet evening at home. "I don't know if you two realize, but today is an important anniversary."

Carly and Jimmy looked at each other wide-eyed. They *never* remembered their parents' wedding anniversary. They felt bad about it, but every single year they forgot to congratulate their parents until they saw the vase of roses Dad had bought for Mom sitting on the kitchen table.

But before they could stammer out a congratulation, Dad went on.

"We've had Chaos for a month. The trial period is over!"

"Oh," Jimmy said. He felt his heart give a little jolt in his chest. "What . . . what does that mean? Do we still have to think about giving her up?"

Mom and Dad both laughed at the same time—until they saw how serious Carly and Jimmy's faces were.

"I think it's pretty clear that Chaos has settled into our family very well," Mom said reassuringly.

"So we can keep her?" Carly and Jimmy both said at the exact same time.

"I think it's the only thing to do now," Dad said.

Jimmy threw his arms around Chaos's neck. By this time, she was so used to the family and to Carly and Jimmy in particular that a sudden gesture like this didn't even make her flinch. She just licked his ear happily.

"But wait," Carly said. "Just for good measure . . . shouldn't we be rational about this decision? Remember how we promised to revisit the Decision-Making Process at the end of the month? We never actually did Step 6."

Mom smiled proudly at Carly. "I think you're absolutely right. It *is* time to revisit the Decision-Making Process. It's clear that we're going to keep Chaos permanently, but keeping her means we're going to have to make some additional decisions about her care. So . . . let's go to the whiteboard?"

As the family gathered around the whiteboard, Jimmy asked, "I can't remember. What's Step 6?"

Carly put on her best teacher voice. "Step 6: *evaluate and adjust* depending on the outcomes."

"Okay," Jimmy said, "so that means we need to identify the outcomes?"

"That's right," Mom agreed. "When we started the Decision-Making Process last month, we didn't know if Chaos would be responsive to training. We didn't know if she would integrate into our family. What do we know now?"

"She *is* trainable!" Carly exclaimed. "It took patience and time, but we've gotten her to take a walk with us. And she's getting more and more used to being around other people and dogs and even cars."

"Right," Mom said. "So if we were to go back to Step 1 of the Decision-Making Process and identify some new future possibilities based on what we now know about Chaos, what might they be?"

"I bet with a little more patience and training, she'll be completely comfortable! We'll even be able to take her to the dog park."

"That's *possible*," Dad said. "But let's be conservative. What's another possibility?"

"It's also possible that this is as far as she's going to get," Carly said.

"I'd agree," Mom said. "Her progress depends on how much the two of you are willing to keep consistently giving her your time and effort and patience and love. But it also depends on Chaos as her own individual dog. She *has* had a lot of history before she ever came to us, and that might mean she has her limits."

"Even if this is as comfortable as she ever gets," Jimmy said, "I still love her and will keep being patient with her."

"Me too," Carly said.

"And so will we," Mom and Dad both agreed.

"Which means," Mom said, "we just analyzed and evaluated the possibilities, and we all came to the same conclusion: We made the right decision adopting Chaos. She is now permanently a part of our family."

Everyone whooped and cheered. Then, just as they had a month before, Dad stuck his hand out into the center of the family circle. Mom stacked hers on top of his, Carly added hers, and Jimmy placed his hand on top. Just for fun, Carly gently picked up Chaos's paw—wrapped in its cast—and added it to the top of the pile.

"Go team!" Dad said.

Chaos, who by now was perfectly accustomed to the family's usual noise and exuberance, barked her agreement.

"But wait, Mom," Carly said, "you said there would be more decisions to make now that Chaos is staying with us permanently."

"That's very true," Mom said. "Remember how we had to set aside some long-term considerations when we first took Chaos in for a trial period? First of all, there's the expense of getting her spayed, which is something we definitely have to do now. And there are any future medical expenses that we can't anticipate. I think we need to go back to Step 3 of the Decision-Making Process—analyze and quantify—to address how we're going to deal with Chaos's ongoing care."

Just as they had done the month before, the family gathered around Dad's iPad to do some research. From Dr. Ancona's website, they found an estimated cost of spaying a dog of Chaos's age.

"Huh," Dad said. "That's not as much as I expected. And we do *have* to make this investment now that we've committed to being responsible pet owners for Chaos."

"I think it's only fair that you two should be involved in this expense," Mom added, "since Chaos is partly your dog and partly your responsibility. But it is more than you can save from your allowance."

"Well," Jimmy said, "I was planning to mow lawns again this summer."

"And I'm already babysitting almost every other week for the Logan family," Carly added. "What if we agree to pay you a percentage of whatever we earn until the spaying is paid for?"

"That's a very fair idea," Dad said. "But how about we say you pay us a percentage of your earnings, until you get to 50 percent of the cost of spaying? After all, Chaos is Mom and my dog, too."

Jimmy and Carly broke into huge smiles. They were delighted to see that their practical, sometimes strict dad had completely turned around about having a dog.

"Deal!" Jimmy and Carly said together.

"Hey, look at this," Dad said, turning back to his iPad. "There's a link on Dr. Ancona's website about pet insurance. It seems worth checking out."

He tapped the link, and the family gathered around to peer over his shoulders at the screen.

"This is pretty interesting, you guys," Mom said. "The whole insurance industry is based on what we've been talking about this month. It's based on risk management. Basically, when you know you are facing a possible *loss*, you can buy insurance to help offset the financial cost to you if that loss happens."

"So," Dad explained, "people who are buying a house know that it's possible that there could be a big storm and a tree could fall on their roof. So they buy homeowner's insurance and pay a certain amount of money every month. It's called a premium. If a tree never falls on their house, well, they don't get their money back. They were paying for peace of mind. But if the tree *does* fall—the insurance company will pay to have the roof fixed, based on its agreement with the homeowners."

"But if the homeowners were only paying a small amount of money each month," Carly wanted to know, "how can the insurance company afford to pay for the roof—especially if it's really expensive?"

"That's a great point," Mom said. "The whole industry works because lots of people participate. So, lots and lots of homeowners pay a premium each month, which adds up to a lot of money. And then, only a relatively small number of people ever actually need to *make a claim*—that means ask for money from the insurance company—so when they do, the insurance company has the money."

"There's actually a whole science around this," Dad said. "It's called *actuarial science*. It's all about trying to calculate how many customers an insurance company needs and how much they need to be paying so that the insurance company can afford to pay for certain losses that may or may not happen."

"And there's all kinds of different insurance," Mom said. "So there are all kinds of people working to understand how often, say, natural disasters happen that might affect homeowners. But also how often medical expenses come up— that's for medical insurance. Or how often car accidents happen and how expensive they are—that's for car insurance. There's also life insurance—to help offset the cost of a funeral and help the family member's survivors with expenses if they suddenly lose the income of a parent or spouse. There's even traveler's insurance, in case the airline loses your luggage or you get sick while you're in a foreign country that doesn't accept your medical insurance."

"And," Dad said, "it looks like there's pet insurance, too! To help people pay if their pets get sick."

"Do you think we should have pet insurance for Chaos?" Carly asked.

"We can make the decision using the same tools for evaluation that actuaries use," Mom said.

"Actuaries," Dad added, "are people who practice actuarial science."

"We know a lot now about risk," Mom said. "But there are actually two kinds of risk. There is *pure risk*, which only has two possible outcomes: *loss* or *no loss*. And there is *speculative risk*, which has three possible outcomes: *loss*, *no loss*, or *gain*."

"How could you ever gain from a risk?" Jimmy asked.

"Well, we gained something when we took a risk on adopting Chaos," Carly said. "We gained a family pet!" "That's exactly right," Mom agreed. "Adopting Chaos was a *speculative risk*. In the end, there was a *gain*—we got a family pet. Of course, that gain wasn't without the financial, time, and effort investment of owning a pet."

"So, what kind of risk would we be facing in terms of whether or not Chaos gets sick and needs medical care in the future?" Dad asked.

Carly and Jimmy paused for a moment.

"That sounds like *pure risk*," Carly said finally. "Either she doesn't get sick—*no loss*. Or she does—*loss*."

"Right again," Mom agreed. "Insurance is all about helping people guard against pure risk. People face situations that either might happen and cause them a loss, or might not happen and cause them no loss. If the situation happens and the family has insurance, then the loss is either reduced or eliminated altogether by the insurance company's contribution."

"So, we're facing the pure risk of whether or not Chaos gets sick . . . but it seems like she probably *will*. I mean, I get a cold a couple times a year at least! And that one time I broke my arm rollerblading," Carly said.

"And I had the chicken pox!" Jimmy piped up.

"It's true," Mom agreed. "When it comes to medical insurance, it's less about whether things will happen and more about how often they will happen and how bad they will be. So those are two concepts we talked about a little before. There's *expected frequency*: How many times can we expect to experience a loss in a given time period—say, the duration of Chaos's life? And there's *expected severity*: When a loss does happen—when Chaos does get sick—how much will it cost us financially? That depends on what kind of illness or injury she gets."

Carly and Jimmy nodded to show that they were following her.

"For the most part, expected frequency and expected severity depend a lot on *random variables*—chance events that may or may not occur. Right? Like, Chaos getting hit by a car before you found her was a *random variable* that meant the *severity* of the cost of adopting her was higher. We had to pay to treat her broken leg."

"Hey!" Jimmy exclaimed. "Aren't *random variables* kind of like *perils* and *hazards*?"

"Yeah, a little," Mom agreed. "Good job remembering. A *peril* is something that could cause a loss—and it might occur randomly. So, a peril might be Chaos getting an illness. And a *hazard* is something that increases the odds of the *peril* happening. So, maybe Chaos happens to be a dog breed that gets sick more easily. That would be a *hazard*."

Here, Dad joined in the conversation. "So actuaries use *statistics*—numerical research about perils and losses that have occurred in the past—to help them determine the *probability* of future outcomes. And that helps them decide how much they should be charging for insurance, so that they know they'll have their customers covered if and when things happen."

"So what *are* they charging?" Carly asked, turning back to the iPad.

The website gave a long list of medical conditions that could possibly befall a dog. It included everything from *arthritis* to *cut or bite wound* to *tumors*. Then it listed different plans, some with more expensive monthly premiums that covered more of the medical conditions, and some with cheaper monthly premiums that covered only the basics.

"How do we decide which plan to pick?" Jimmy asked. "We can't predict what she'll need!"

"I say we go back to the Decision-Making Process," Mom suggested. "Let's use Step 3: analyze and quantify. We can all ask our friends with pets what kind of conditions they've faced. We can do some online searching to see what conditions we might expect dogs of Chaos's breed to get as they age—we know she's got some sheep dog and mastiff in her. And then we factor in what we can afford as a family. If it's not full coverage, then we take a leap of faith."

"But wait," Carly—always the practical one—said. "You've been emphasizing all this time, Mom, that we can't predict the future 100 percent. So, what if we get a plan that covers the most expected conditions, and then something random happens, something unpredictable, and we're not covered? How do people prepare for the unpredictable?"

Mom laughed. "If you ever find a sure-fire answer to that question," she said, "you'll be the richest woman on the planet. There are almost always 'outlier' events that occur outside the normally arrayed distribution of a bell curve. Actuaries are actually taught to accommodate for this by factoring in what's called a *risk charge*—a little bit of cushion built into the premium to ensure that customers are still covered in case of an error in estimation and calculation."

Carly nodded, but it was clear she wasn't quite convinced.

"Here's the thing," Mom said. "Even though human beings have this powerful capacity to be disciplined, and to use statistical, quantitative, *objective* data and facts to come to decisions . . . all of us, even the most rational of us, have a natural tendency to veer toward the easiest course of action. So, in terms of decision making, we feel this strong tug toward the less structured process of 'going with your gut' or following the advice of junk science that might be easier to grasp but isn't necessarily based in facts."

Carly nodded slowly. She was following what her mother was saying—but didn't yet see how it connected to her question.

"So, a lot of people, when they are shopping for insurance, are shopping emotionally. Of course, buying insurance is a really sound, rational decision to make—but it's also something that just makes us *feel* better. It makes us feel more secure. It has what I call *worry value*—which means it helps to reduce worry about exactly those outlier events that can't be predicted.

"And everyone has a different threshold of worry value—based on their subjective experiences, everyone has a different level of risk and uncertainty that they are willing to tolerate. When we buy insurance, we can think rationally about what the best plan is for us and for Chaos, but a part of the process will also be to factor in: *Which plan will most reduce our worry value?*"

"Okay," Carly said. "That makes sense to me. This all goes back to what we've been saying all along. In decision-making, the objective and the subjective always go hand-in-hand. They both play a role."

"Exactly," Mom agreed. "It's just human nature."

"It sounds like it's time to get started," Jimmy said. "Should we divide up the research and then make a decision tomorrow night?"

"It's a plan!" Mom and Dad agreed, and the whole family busily split off to their computers to start researching.

CHAPTER 11

Mom and Dad, do you think the person who hit Chaos with their car realized that they hit her?" Jimmy asked. It was the following evening, and the family was gathered in the living room snacking on a bowl of popcorn and finishing up their whiteboard decision about pet insurance. They had managed to find a mid-level plan that covered most of the conditions they had most cause to worry about Chaos developing—*and* would also cover her spaying surgery. Using the whiteboard, Carly, Jimmy, and their parents had agreed on a schedule of payment so that Carly and Jimmy would use their allowance and parts of their earnings from babysitting and lawn mowing to help pay the monthly insurance premium.

Once everything was agreed upon, they had settled into a contented silence, watching Chaos as she dozed on the carpet at their feet.

Jimmy's question had cast a pall over the room.

Dad thought it over for a moment and then said gravely, "It's hard to imagine they didn't. Chaos is a pretty big dog. They had to have seen her."

"Then why didn't they stop and help her?" Carly exclaimed.

Again, Mom and Dad were both silent for a moment.

Finally, Mom spoke. "We'll never have any way of knowing what was going through their minds. But my guess is . . . well, people rarely act just out of malice—just out of a desire to cause harm. More often, when they do things that hurt other people—or, in this case, an animal—they're acting out of fear and ignorance."

"What would they have to be afraid of?" Jimmy said. "*They're* the ones who hit Chaos. *She* was the one who had a reason to be afraid."

"True," Dad said. "But maybe they were speeding or ran a stop sign and were afraid of getting in trouble for it."

"Or," Mom added, "maybe they were acting out of ignorance."

"What do you mean?" Carly asked. "Ignorance means that you don't know or understand something. So, what could they have been ignorant of?"

"Maybe they were ignorant of how to think—and feel— through the consequences of their actions," Mom said. "You guys know what the word *empathy* means, right?"

"I think so," Jimmy said. "It's when you can put yourself in someone else's shoes and understand what they're feeling."

"Right," Mom said. "It's a little different from *sympathy*, which means that you feel *for* someone—you feel sorry for them. When you have *empathy*, you feel *with* them—you seek to understand their experience. It's a really important part of being a loving, compassionate, fair member of society. And it's also really hard. Not everyone has learned how to do it—and people who haven't often make poor decisions, decisions that don't take other people into account."

"Your mom's right," Dad jumped in. As a principal at a middle school, the concept of empathy was near and dear to him. Pretty much all of the behavioral problems he encountered among his students stemmed in some way from failures of empathy.

"Empathy is actually a great decision-making tool," Dad continued. "When we are able to put ourselves in someone else's shoes, it helps us see the ramifications of our actions. And it also helps us think more creatively—sometimes we come up with solutions that wouldn't have occurred to us if we were only thinking of our own needs and desires."

"So," Carly said slowly, "I still don't understand why the people who hit Chaos wouldn't have stopped and helped her. You say empathy is hard, but it seems obvious to me—if they hurt an animal, how could they not wonder if she was okay and try to do something to help her?"

"That's not an easy question," Dad sad. "Remember how we all realized that there was a lot going on under Lonnie's rude behavior than we could ever have guessed? We'll probably never know why the driver who hit Chaos didn't stop—why they didn't have empathy for Chaos."

"I do have some ideas, though," Mom added, "about what underlies a lot of people's ignorance. The difficult truth is that making sound decisions is really hard work. I mean, think about how much time and effort we've spent on our whiteboard decisions in the last few weeks. It would have been much easier to just act on gut instinct and impulse."

"True," Jimmy said. "But then we might have made the wrong decision! Chaos might have stayed at the shelter and gotten euthanized."

"Exactly," Mom said. "So, the hard work is worth it. But when we're in the thick of an emotional decision, we don't always realize that it's worth it. We feel overwhelmed and we just want to choose the first and easiest option available. I think most ignorance is rooted in the weakness of our undisciplined minds. Disciplined, conscientious decision-making takes so much more energy."

Just at that moment, the doorbell rang. Carly jumped up to answer the door. There, on the front porch, were Lonnie and his mother, Abigail, a petite woman with a short brown bob. She was holding a baking tray covered in tinfoil.

"Hi there, Carly!" She exclaimed brightly. "I've heard so much about you and your brother from Lonnie."

Lonnie grinned sheepishly. "We had some leftover brownies, and since Mom hasn't met you guys yet, I suggested we bring them over here."

Carly smiled a little shyly.

"Are—are you guys busy right now?" Lonnie asked.

"No!" Carly exclaimed. "Not at all! Come in, please."

Carly brought Lonnie and his mother into the living room to join the rest of the family. Everyone introduced themselves to Lonnie's mom—except, of course, Pete, who already knew her well from having been Lonnie's principal. Then, they uncovered the tray of warm, gooey brownies and dug in.

"How is Chaos doing?" Lonnie asked as everyone munched away happily on their brownies.

Almost as if in reply, Chaos left the corner of the room where she had been resting and went trotting over to Lonnie to burrow her head into his leg. He broke into a wide grin and gave her a scratch behind the ears.

"She's been doing better and better!" Jimmy said. "Thanks to you, and helping us with positive reinforcement, she's getting more used to the neighborhood and to people."

"And her cast is going to come off pretty soon," Carly said. "Dr. Ancona—that's her vet—thinks she'll be as good as new. Won't even have a limp."

"That's great!" Lonnie exclaimed. Then, his expression changed. "It's just awful that she had to go through this in the first place. Who would hit a dog with their car and then just leave her there, without trying to help?"

Carly and Jimmy were both quiet for a moment. They thought it was better not to remind Lonnie that he himself had suggested leaving the dog to die when they had first found her. Clearly, he had not been himself when he'd said it. Maybe he was even speaking from ignorance and fear—as Carly and Jimmy's parents had just talked about.

"You know," Lonnie's mom Abigail said thoughtfully, "I'm pretty sure there are security cameras at some of the intersections in this neighborhood. There's a private security company that our homeowners' association hired to keep the neighborhood safe. It was something the realtor mentioned to me as a bonus when I was thinking about buying our house."

"You mean," Lonnie said, "that maybe there's video evidence of who did it?"

Abigail made a non-committal expression. "I don't want to get anyone's hopes up," she said. "We don't know *where* Chaos got hit—sometimes injured animals travel quite a distance to find a hiding spot. And even if she was hit in the neighborhood, we don't know if it happened in range of a security camera."

"True," Jimmy and Carly's dad agreed. "And we don't know whether the camera would have captured a license plate number."

"But . . . what if it *did*? Like, what if we had video evidence of what happened, and could link the car to the driver?" Jimmy said, his voice building with excitement.

"Yeah," Lonnie said, catching onto Jimmy's fervor. "We might be able to get justice for Chaos. If that person had to go to court or pay a fine or whatever the law says, they might be more likely to drive safer in the future. Or at least stop and help if an accident *does* happen."

"Wait, that's not all!" Carly exclaimed. "If we find the person and bring them to justice, we could write a letter to the editor of the city newspaper about it! And then who knows how many more people would learn something. It's just like

Mom was talking about earlier—it would be a way of spreading empathy and counteracting ignorance!"

All three parents were smiling in spite of themselves.

"Listen, I don't see why not," Abigail said. "At least, it couldn't hurt to try. As long as you don't get your hopes up too much. These things can be harder than you expect to uncover."

"Agreed," Dad said. "It might be hard to convince the security company to review the footage, and if they do, it might be hard to convince the police to respond. They've got a lot on their plates, and unfortunately, dogs with broken legs might not be a high priority."

"But we think you're right that it's worth trying," Mom finished earnestly.

"Tell you what," Dad said, "it's past business hours now, so there's no point trying to contact the security company. But tomorrow, I'll call the neighborhood homeowners' association and find out how to contact them. Once we get a number for them, I'll let you kids take it from there."

Jimmy looked a little wary all of a sudden. "Well . . . what do we say to them?"

"Just tell them your story. That you found an injured dog and the vet is pretty sure she was struck by a car. You're trying to see if you can bring the driver to justice. Ask them politely, and see if they're willing to help you. How does that sound?"

"Deal!" Carly, Jimmy, and Lonnie all spoke at once.

▬ ▬ ▬

"I'm sorry, kids, this is just a pretty unusual request," the customer service representative at the security company, whose name was Marge, was saying.

Carly, Jimmy, and Lonnie were all gathered around the speakerphone on the desk in Kim's home office. They had explained to Marge that they were hoping to get the security company to review its footage of the neighborhood streets for a dog strike that probably occurred during the night before their first day of school.

"We largely keep surveillance footage of the neighborhood to assist police in case there's a home break. Reviewing that much footage—especially if you're not sure where the incident occurred and which camera might have captured it—would take a lot of man hours. It would be very expensive."

Jimmy looked stricken. But suddenly, Lonnie's face brightened. He repeated a magic phrase that he had heard his mother use when she needed a little extra help.

"Is there a manager that we might be able to speak to?" Lonnie said, in a very polite and adult voice.

Marge paused and sighed. She was clearly feeling a little taxed by this conversation.

"All right," she said. "I'll get him on the line. Hold please."

After a buzz and a moment of static, hold music came over the line.

"What are you going to say?" Carly asked, turning to Lonnie wide-eyed.

Lonnie shrugged. "I don't actually know. I guess just repeat the same thing, and hope the manager cares more and is willing to help."

Just as Lonnie stopped speaking, the hold music cut off abruptly and a woman's voice came over the line.

"This is Andrea Schultz," she said, "Regional Manager. I understand I'm on the line with Carly, Jim, and Leonard?"

"Lonnie," Lonnie corrected her firmly.

"My apologies, Lonnie," Andrea said, a smile in her voice. "I understand our representative Marge wasn't able to assist you. I hope I'll be able to help. What seems to be your concern?"

Lonnie took a deep breath and then launched into the story.

"We live in the Stony Brook Farms neighborhood, where you have surveillance cameras," he said, "and we're hoping you can help us find some footage that might have captured a crime."

"Oh," Andrea said, sounding concerned. "We haven't had a police report in that neighborhood in years. Has it not been filed yet?"

"Well," Carly said, "we don't have a police report. See . . ." she trailed off, unsure how to explain.

Jimmy jumped in. "My sister Carly and I found an injured dog on the morning of August 24th. The vet is pretty sure she was hit by a car. We'd like to use your security footage to see if we can . . ." Jimmy trailed off, looking for the right word.

"Apprehend the perpetrator," Lonnie finished confidently. Jimmy gave Lonnie a grateful look. Those crime investigation shows Lonnie was hooked on seemed to have a real-life pay-off, at least in terms of Lonnie's vocabulary.

There was a long pause on the other end of the line.

"I see," Andrea said at last. "Listen, folks. What Marge told you is true. You're making a very costly request. It's true that it sounds like a crime has occurred, but in terms of our priorities, this is low on the list."

"But—" Jimmy started.

Before he could continue, Andrea cut in. "I'm afraid there's an even greater difficulty, though. We have limited storage for our surveillance footage. We destroy footage a month out. It's well over a month after August 24th."

Carly, Jimmy, and Lonnie fell silent, a sense of defeat passing over them.

"I'm afraid there really is nothing we can do for you," Andrea said, her voice not unkind. "I'm sorry to hear about the dog. Is she going to be okay?"

"Yes," Carly said, trying to brighten her voice. "Her leg was broken, but she's great now. We adopted her."

"You guys are clearly really good kids," Andrea said. "I bet your parents are very proud of you."

"Thank you," all three of them said quietly.

"I'm sorry I can't be of more help. Good luck with your dog," Andrea said. There was a brief clicking on the line, and then the dial tone sounded.

Carly, Jimmy, and Lonnie all leaned back into their chairs.

"I didn't think it would go that way," Lonnie said.

"Me neither," Jimmy agreed, his voice low.

"We did know it was a long shot," Carly said, "but I'm really disappointed."

Jimmy got up, sighing. "Come on, guys," he said gamely. "Let's try to shake it off. Wanna go take Chaos for a walk?"

"Sure," Lonnie said.

Still feeling crestfallen, the three of them went off to find Chaos.

CHAPTER 12

As Carly, Jimmy, and Lonnie were biking home from school the following afternoon, Carly suddenly slammed on the brakes and brought her bike to an abrupt standstill.

Jimmy and Lonnie pulled up short next to her.

"What's wrong, what's wrong?" Jimmy asked, scared.

"Nothing, I just . . ." Carly trailed off for a moment. Her eyes were fixed on the dog park across the street.

Since it was the afternoon and many people were just getting off of work or school, it was pretty full. A Bernese mountain dog was sitting on his haunches near the gate, happily receiving a scratch from his owner, a woman still wearing a business suit and heels. Three medium-sized dogs were competing for control of a baseball, as they circled around the perimeter of the park, and a couple of small fluffy pups were sniffing shyly at each other. One owner, a young guy in a baseball cap, was throwing a tennis ball for his chocolate lab, and a boxer was tearing along behind the lab trying to steal the ball. It was a happy scene of relaxed people and joyful, exuberant dogs.

Jimmy and Lonnie watched Carly curiously.

"What are you thinking, Carly?" Lonnie asked. "What's going on?"

"Just look how many people with dogs live in this area," Carly said thoughtfully, her eyes fixed on the dog park. "I wonder if . . ." She trailed off again.

"What?" Jimmy pressed finally.

"Well," Carly said, clearly working an idea out in her mind even as she spoke. "We weren't able to get justice for Chaos. But maybe that's not actually the important thing. What's important is the outcome for Chaos, right? And now she is safe and healthy and has a real home. She doesn't care what happens to the driver who hit her—or to her former owner, for that matter. She's just interested in the here and now. And her new here and now is a happy one."

Jimmy nodded. "That's a really good point," he said. "She doesn't even know we were trying to get that footage. We're the ones who feel disappointed about it—not Chaos."

"Yeah," Carly said. "So then . . . I was looking at the dogs in the park, and seeing how all of them are so happy playing with their owners and with other dogs. And thinking . . . what dogs really care about is the present moment."

Jimmy and Lonnie were both hanging on Carly's words, curious where this was going.

"So, if the present moment is what matters most to dogs, and we really want to be helpful to Chaos and to dogs like her . . . then maybe we were focusing on the wrong things by trying to go back in time and find out what happened in the past," Carly said.

"Maybe," she continued, "we could help dogs who are in the situation Chaos *used* to be in. Who don't have a chance at a good home and a loving family. Maybe we could help them to have a better future."

"What do you mean?" Lonnie asked. "Like, what could we actually do for them?"

"I'm not exactly sure what I mean . . ." Carly said. "It's just the start of an idea, that's all."

"It's a good start," Lonnie said. "I like what you're thinking. I just don't know how we can find dogs that need help—and what we could do for them."

"I know how we can figure out the rest of the idea," Jimmy said brightly.

Both Carly and Lonnie turned to look at him curiously.

Jimmy grinned. "Let's go to the whiteboard!"

— — —

"All right," Carly said to Lonnie, "our mom showed us this way of breaking down hard problems into manageable steps. It's called the Six Steps of Risk Management."

She had set up the whiteboard and was jotting, "Step 1," across the top in bold capital letters.

"Why *risk management*?" Lonnie wanted to know. "What are we risking?"

"Well, that's kind of what we'll figure out as we go through the process," Carly said. "Step 1 is to identify the problem we're trying to solve."

Lonnie thought for a moment. "Well, last night it seemed like the problem was that we can't find and apprehend the person who hit Chaos." He thought for a moment. "But based on what you said as we were riding home from school . . . I'm not so sure that *is* a problem anymore. Chaos is safe and has a home—that's what matters most. So, maybe the problem is solved."

"But," Jimmy said, "maybe Carly identified a new problem. Maybe the problem now is that there are lots more dogs in Chaos's situation—who need happy, safe homes and don't have them."

"Right!" Carly said. "That's the problem we're trying to solve." She jotted it down on the board. Then she continued to explain to Lonnie, "In Step 1, we need to identify possible actions we could take—and what their outcomes might be. Then we go through a step-by-step process of evaluating those actions and make a decision about how to proceed."

"Okay," Lonnie said, "I think I see. So, we need to come up with some ideas for things we could do to help dogs like Chaos?"

"Exactly," Jimmy said.

"Well, first we would have to start by finding the dogs that need help. How do we even go about finding dogs that don't have a home?" Lonnie asked.

Suddenly, Jimmy sat bolt upright in his chair. "The shelter!" He exclaimed. "We don't actually have to start from zero with this problem. The county already has a system for identifying and catching stray dogs—the animal control department. *And* they also do their best to find dogs that are being mistreated and get them out of bad homes."

Carly nodded enthusiastically. "You're right. We *don't* have to start from zero—the county has already solved part of the problem."

"Except," Jimmy said gravely, "the shelter euthanizes. *That's* the real problem we're facing. When we first found Chaos, we wanted to help her, so we followed the system the county has in place—we called animal control. And then that created a whole new problem—that she might get euthanized."

"So, that's the problem!" Lonnie exclaimed. "We need to figure out how to help dogs at the shelter that are at risk of being put down."

"That's it, that's it!" Carly exclaimed. "We need to find a way to get the shelter to convert to a "*no-kill*" policy!"

Both Lonnie and Jimmy whooped.

"Carly, that's brilliant!" Lonnie said. Then suddenly he stopped. "But how the heck do we do *that*?"

"That's what we use the Decision-Making Process for!" Carly exclaimed. "Step 1, we identify the problem and possible courses of action. Step 2, we identify subjective and objective risks. Step 3, we analyze and quantify the possibilities. Step 4, we rank the possibilities. Step 5, we make a choice. And then in Step 6, we come back after the fact and evaluate our choice based on what has happened in the real world."

"Slow down, slow down!" Lonnie exclaimed. "I'm new to this, remember?"

"All right, let's stick with Step 1," Jimmy said. "We've figured out the problem. What are some possible courses of action? One possibility is always *inaction*. We don't have to do anything."

"Well, in that case," Lonnie said, "dogs will keep getting euthanized, and we won't be making things better."

"Okay, great," Carly said. "So you've identified a possible course of action—and the likely outcome of that action. Now think about whether you know *objectively* that inaction won't make things better. Is that a conclusion based on facts and data? Or is it something you know *subjectively*? Is it more based on your feelings and prior experience?"

"Huh," Lonnie said. "Good question. I think it's actually a little of both. I mean, we do know for sure that the shelter will keep euthanizing—that's their policy. That's a fact. But when I said, 'It won't make things better,' that was a subjective feeling. That was my own subjective feeling about what 'better' means."

"Exactly!" Carly said. "So, if we want to make a sound, rational decision, we have to get clear about when we're being influenced by facts and when we're being influenced by our emotions. Both can play a role in our final decision, but if we don't clearly separate them, then we won't be able to make a rational choice. That's what Step 2, considering the subjective and objective factors, is all about."

"Okay, so here's a thought," Jimmy jumped in. "*Why* does the shelter euthanize dogs? Remember what both Hank the animal control specialist and Eve the shelter manager kept saying? The shelter has 'limited resources.'"

"Money," Lonnie said. "It all boils down to money. They don't have enough money to take care of all the dogs they find."

Carly and Jimmy both thought for a moment. Lonnie was right. Without more money to help feed and care for more dogs, there was no way the animal shelter would be able to change its policy.

"So, that gives us another possible course of action," Carly said.

"What?" Both Lonnie and Jimmy asked together.

"We raise money for the shelter."

Jimmy's eyebrows shot up. "That's such a cool idea!" He exclaimed. "Except . . . I don't even know where we'd start."

"Well," Carly said slowly, turning back to the whiteboard where she had been taking notes. "I think this is where Step 3—analyze and quantify—really comes into play. We need to find out from the shelter exactly how much it costs to take care of a dog, how many dogs they tend to receive, how often they get adopted . . ."

"Exactly," Lonnie agreed, "if we can get those numbers, we can calculate how much we would need to help the shelter keep operating with a lot more dogs to take care of."

Jimmy sank back into his chair. "That's, like . . . a *really* hard question. I don't know how to figure out budgets. I don't know how to fundraise. How are we ever going to *do* this?"

"Well, remember what Mom said about fear and ignorance?" Carly asked. "I think that's standing in our way right now. It's giving you the *subjective* feeling that this is impossible. The more we can get informed, the more options might open themselves up to us."

Lonnie had been sitting quietly, listening to them with a thoughtful expression. Now, he broke in. "Guys," he said, "we don't have to do this by ourselves! My mom is the executive assistant at a non-profit."

"What's a non-profit?" Jimmy asked.

"It's like a business," Lonnie said, "but the point isn't to make money—to make a profit. The point is just to fulfill the organization's mission. Usually non-profits do something that helps people or is good for society in some way. So, my mom's organization, for example, raises money for cancer research."

Carly and Jimmy were listening very carefully.

"Maybe she could help give us some ideas about raising money for the shelter," Lonnie said.

"That's perfect!" Carly exclaimed.

"Is your mom home right now?" Jimmy asked. "Do you think she'd be willing to come over and help us?"

"Of course!" Lonnie said. "I bet she'd be happy to."

"I'll go ask her," Jimmy said, jumping up. "That way Carly can keep explaining the Decision-Making Process to you."

"Awesome," Lonnie said. Jimmy was already rushing out of the living room toward the front door.

Standing breathlessly on Lonnie's front porch, Jimmy explained to Lonnie's mom in a flood of words what the three of them were trying to do. Abigail listened carefully, and by the time Jimmy got to the end of his explanation, she was smiling widely.

"Jimmy," she said, "I think this is a wonderful idea. Not only do you have the potential to help a lot of dogs, you'll also be doing something good for families that would like to adopt a pet. *And*, you, Lonnie, and Carly will learn a lot about what it's like to run an organization."

Jimmy nodded enthusiastically. "Right!" He exclaimed. "I think we could really make a difference."

"I think so too," Abigail agreed. "And I'd be honored to help you. Let's go."

As she and Jimmy walked across her front lawn back to Jimmy and Carly's house, Abigail stopped suddenly and put a hand on Jimmy's shoulder.

"Listen, Jimmy," she said solemnly, "I want to thank you—and Carly—for being so kind to Lonnie. I think you know that our family hasn't had a very easy year. It was particularly hard on Lonnie, and he has been really struggling. But ever since he met you and Carly, he's been doing so much better. He's engaged in school, he's kinder to his peers, and for the first time in a long time, he seems excited about and hopeful about his life and his future."

Jimmy smiled somewhat bashfully. He shrugged his shoulders. "Well, we like Lonnie a lot. We're happy he wanted to be friends with us."

Abigail returned Jimmy's smile. "And he's happy you wanted to be friends with him. So am I. You've given him a real sense of belonging. Thank you," she said again.

Then, the two of them continued on in silence. As they walked, it suddenly occurred to Jimmy that, even though Abigail wasn't aware of it, they had just completed Step 6 of the Decision-Making Process in terms of the whiteboard decision to befriend Lonnie. Abigail had just unknowingly helped Jimmy evaluate the outcome of his and Carly's decision. And it had turned out to be the right one.

EPILOGUE

I t was a Tuesday afternoon, and Jimmy and Lonnie were manning their stand at the entrance of the dog park while Carly played fetch with Chaos nearby.

After working with Abigail and with Eve at the animal shelter, they had created a budget that would allow the shelter, over the course of three years, to convert entirely to a *"no-kill"* policy. The plan involved several facets. The shelter had begun collaborating with local farms and sanctuaries to create placements for dogs that were difficult to adopt into family homes. And, Carly, Jimmy, and Lonnie's fundraising efforts would allow the shelter to expand its space so that it could take in more dogs and keep them longer.

Most importantly, however, the fundraising would give the shelter more resources to reach out to the community to get dogs adopted. This outreach would include a social media presence that would advertise adoptable dogs to the community, as well as regular "dog fairs" at local libraries and pet stores, where families could come and meet dogs in need of a home.

Abigail had helped set up a system for fundraising that involved reaching out to donors in the community who cared about animal welfare. Another big part of the plan was a stand that Carly, Jimmy, and Lonnie had set up at the dog park.

As they had been brainstorming on the whiteboard about how to help the shelter convert to a no-kill policy, Abigail had suggested that the kids come up with a product to sell, and donate the profits to the shelter. The question was, what kind of product for dogs would always be in demand?

As soon as Abigail had posed the question, a light bulb went on in Jimmy's mind.

"Baseballs and tennis balls!" He exclaimed.

It was the perfect idea. There was a built-in customer base at the dog park of people in need—right then and there—of balls to throw for their dogs. Dog owners & lovers could donate new baseballs and tennis balls—as they are cheap to buy in bulk at sporting goods stores or "on-line," which could be resold at the park for a profit. And, since dogs are always quick to tear any ball to shreds, there was never a shortage of demand.

So, every Tuesday afternoon after school, Carly, Jimmy, and Lonnie set up a little stand at the dog park where they sold tennis balls for a dollar and baseballs for two bucks. One hundred percent of the money they made went back to the shelter to help complete their three-year plan of phasing out euthanasia.

Today, Jimmy and Lonnie were manning the stand while Carly tossed a ball with Chaos.

Just as Dr. Ancona had predicted, Chaos was completely healed. Her formerly broken leg was better than ever. But even more importantly, the love and acceptance she had experienced as a member of Carly and Jimmy's family had helped her to completely overcome the fear and anxiety she had experienced in her early life.

She was so used to other dogs—and people—that she could play at the dog park completely comfortably. On a regular basis, she could be seen rolling on her back in the grass, surrounded by other dogs. When Carly and Jimmy took her on walks through the neighborhood, she held her head high, and no longer flinched when cars drove by. It was as if she had never had an accident at all.

As Chaos began to wear herself out running back and forth playing fetch with Carly, the two of them wandered slowly back to the tennis ball and baseball stand to join Lonnie and Jimmy. Chaos lay down contentedly in the grass at their feet. Just then, Carly and Jimmy's mom strolled into the dog park.

"How are you guys doing?" She called as she approached. "I was just out for a walk and thought I'd stop by and check in."

"It's going great, Mom!" Jimmy exclaimed. "We met our earnings goal for the week—and I think we're going to go about 10 percent over!"

"That's wonderful," Mom said. "You know; you guys have done a really outstanding job. You're making a real difference in the lives of dogs—and families—in this community, and not only that, but you're becoming successful businesspeople in your own right."

Carly, Jimmy, and Lonnie all beamed.

"You know what my favorite thing about what you've done is?" Mom asked.

"What?" Asked Jimmy.

"You just did it."

The three kids all must have looked a little confused, because Mom laughed.

"One of the trickiest things about making a decision is often Step 5—make a choice *and act on it*. Sometimes, we have all the information we need, we've thought about the risks . . . but then we get stuck thinking and over thinking the possible outcomes. Some people like to call it 'paralysis by over-analysis.' We just can't seem to move forward because we're waiting for circumstances to be perfect before we take the plunge."

"But that's just it!" Carly exclaimed. "The circumstances will *never* be perfect. That's the most important thing I've learned about the Decision-Making Process. There are always going to be uncertainties. We're always going to face risk, and we can never be absolutely certain of the future, even when we've taken all the steps to think things through. So . . . at the end of the day, we just can't be perfectionists."

"Yeah!" Jimmy agreed. "We didn't know for sure what would happen when we adopted Chaos. And we also didn't know for sure what would happen when we decided to help the shelter raise funds. But we *did* think things through carefully— and then we finally came to a point where, like you said, Mom, it was time to *just do it*."

"As far as I'm concerned," Lonnie said, "it seems like risk & uncertainty are always going to be a part of life. There's no way to avoid them. But there *are* ways to prepare for risk and uncertainty. And I've learned from all of this that taking risks—as long as you've thought them through—is worth it."

"Right!" Jimmy and Carly said at the exact same moment.

Chaos lifted her huge, furry head and gave a happy bark of agreement.

ABOUT THE AUTHOR

Gary is the founder and Managing Partner of **The Miller Financial Group**, a 2nd generation Independent Property & Casualty Insurance, Financial Services & Risk Management Based Consulting Practice, established in the historic Ft. Washington and Spring House, PA areas, practicing for over 68 years.

Gary started his career in insurance over 35 years ago, joining his father's long standing and successful insurance practice which was founded in 1948. Gary's father Ray Miller, founder of **Miller Insurance Associates**, served in community and formerly held the position of President, Upper Dublin

Township Board of Commissioners. Gary has continued to this day to be active in local community in Upper Dublin Township.

Growing up and living in Upper Dublin Township for over 60 years, Gary & his family have lived in Dresher, PA. Gary graduated from Upper Dublin High School and is a graduate of West Point. Gary was commissioned as a 2nd Lieutenant in the Field Artillery, having earned his BS in Engineering from the United States Military Academy at West Point, NY, serving over 20 years in military service, both active and reserve, with the US Army. Gary earned his MBA in Risk Management from the Fox School of Business, Temple University & served as an Adjunct Professor for 10 years within the Department of Risk, Insurance, Healthcare Management & Actuarial Sciences, which is currently ranked as a leading undergraduate program by US News & World Report. Gary is a current member of the Dean's Council, Fox School of Business, Temple University, and has attained the professional insurance industry designation as a Certified Insurance Counselor, (CIC).

Gary has been active with the Pennsylvania Independent Insurance Agents and Brokers Association (IIA&B) out of Harrisburg, PA, a professional insurance trade association for independent agents and brokers.

Gary is a past recipient of the Upper Dublin Township's Citizen of the Year & current member of the Upper Dublin High School Athletic Hall of Fame. He has been active in his local parish church and has coached at many levels in football, basketball & baseball. Gary & his wife Carol have lived in Upper Dublin, raising 3 children, all married, currently with 7 grandchildren.

A free eBook edition is available with the purchase of this book.

To claim your free eBook edition:

1. Download the Shelfie app.
2. Write your name in upper case in the box.
3. Use the Shelfie app to submit a photo.
4. Download your eBook to any device.

Shelfie

A **free** eBook edition is available
with the purchase of this print book.

CLEARLY PRINT YOUR NAME ABOVE IN UPPER CASE

Instructions to claim your free eBook edition:
1. Download the Shelfie app for Android or iOS
2. Write your name in **UPPER CASE** above
3. Use the Shelfie app to submit a photo
4. Download your eBook to any device

Print & Digital Together Forever.

Snap a photo

Free eBook

Read anywhere

The Morgan James
Speakers Group

www.TheMorganJamesSpeakersGroup.com

We connect Morgan James published
authors with live and online events
and audiences whom will benefit
from their expertise.

 Morgan James makes all of our titles available
through the Library for All Charity Organization.

www.LibraryForAll.org